Congressional
Research
Service

# Taiwan: Major U.S. Arms Sales Since 1990

Shirley A. Kan
Specialist in Asian Security Affairs

May 21, 2012

Congressional Research Service

7-5700

www.crs.gov

RL30957

**CRS Report for Congress**
*Prepared for Members and Committees of Congress*

# Summary

This report, updated as warranted, discusses U.S. security assistance to Taiwan, or Republic of China (ROC), including policy issues for Congress and legislation. Congress has oversight of the Taiwan Relations Act (TRA), P.L. 96-8, which has governed arms sales to Taiwan since 1979, when the United States recognized the People's Republic of China (PRC) instead of the ROC. Two other relevant parts of the "one China" policy are the August 17, 1982, U.S.-PRC Joint Communique and the "Six Assurances" to Taiwan. U.S. arms sales to Taiwan have been significant. The United States also expanded military ties with Taiwan after the PRC's missile firings in 1995-1996. However, the U.S.-ROC Mutual Defense Treaty terminated in 1979.

At the last U.S.-Taiwan annual arms sales talks on April 24, 2001, President George W. Bush approved for possible sale diesel-electric submarines, P-3 anti-submarine warfare (ASW) aircraft (linked to the submarine sale), four decommissioned U.S. Kidd-class destroyers, and other items. Bush also deferred decisions on Aegis-equipped destroyers and other items, while denying other requests. Afterward, attention turned to Taiwan, where the military, civilian officials, and legislators from competing political parties debated contentious issues about how much to spend on defense and which U.S. weapons to acquire, despite the increasing threat (including a missile buildup) from the People's Liberation Army (PLA). The Pentagon also has broadened its concern from Taiwan's arms purchases to its defense spending, seriousness in self-defense and protection of secrets, joint capabilities, operational readiness, critical infrastructure protection, and innovative, asymmetrical advantages. Blocked by the Kuomintang (KMT) party in the Legislative Yuan (LY) that opposed the Democratic Progressive Party (DPP)'s president (2000-2008), the Special Budget (not passed) for submarines, P-3C ASW aircraft, and PAC-3 missile defense systems was cut from $18 billion in 2004 to $9 billion (for submarines only) in 2005. In March 2006, Taiwan's defense minister requested a 2006 Supplemental Defense Budget (not passed) in part for submarine procurement, P-3Cs, and PAC-2 upgrades (not new PAC-3 missiles). In June 2007, the LY passed Taiwan's 2007 defense budget with funds for P-3C planes, PAC-2 upgrades, and F-16C/D fighters. In December 2007, the LY approved $62 million to start the sub design phase. After the KMT's Ma Ying-jeou became President in May 2008, he resumed cross-strait talks while retaining the arms requests. But he cut the defense budget until an increase in 2012.

Attention also turned to U.S. decisions on pending arms sales. In 2008, congressional concerns mounted about a suspected "freeze" in President Bush's notifications to Congress on arms sales. On October 3, 2008, Bush finally notified Congress. However, he submitted six of the eight pending programs (not a "package") for a combined value of $6.5 billion.

Despite the concerns in 2008, President Obama repeated that cycle to wait to submit formal notifications for congressional review all at one time (on January 29, 2010) of five major programs with a total value of $6.4 billion and again (on September 21, 2011) of three major programs with a total value of $5.9 billion, including upgrades for Taiwan's existing F-16A/B fighters. Like Bush, President Obama did not notify the submarine design program (the only one pending from decisions in 2001) and has not accepted Taiwan's formal request for new F-16C/D fighters (pending since 2006).

Legislation in the 112th Congress includes H.Con.Res. 39 (Andrews), H.R. 2583 (Ros-Lehtinen), S. 1539 (Cornyn), H.R. 2918 (Ros-Lehtinen), H.R. 2992 (Granger), and H.R. 4310 (McKeon). See "Major Congressional Action" for details and other congressional actions.

# Contents

# U.S. Policy

This CRS Report discusses U.S. security assistance for Taiwan, formally called the Republic of China (ROC), particularly policy issues for Congress. It also lists sales of major defense articles and services to Taiwan, as approved by the President and notified to Congress since 1990. This report uses a variety of unclassified consultations and citations in the United States and Taiwan.

## Role of Congress

Congress passed and exercises oversight of the Taiwan Relations Act (TRA), P.L. 96-8, the law that has governed U.S. arms sales to Taiwan since 1979, when the United States recognized the People's Republic of China (PRC) instead of the ROC. The TRA specifies that it is U.S. policy, among the stipulations: to consider any nonpeaceful means to determine Taiwan's future "a threat" to the peace and security of the Western Pacific and of "grave concern" to the United States; "to provide Taiwan with arms of a defensive character;" and "to maintain the capacity of the United States to resist any resort to force or other forms of coercion" jeopardizing the security, or social or economic system of Taiwan's people. Section 3(a) states that "the United States will make available to Taiwan such defense articles and defense services in such quantity as may be necessary to enable Taiwan to maintain a sufficient self-defense capability." The TRA specifies a congressional role in decision-making on security assistance for Taiwan. Section 3(b) stipulates that the President and Congress shall determine the nature and quantity of such defense articles and services "based solely" upon their judgment of the needs of Taiwan, in accordance with procedures established by law. Section 3(b) also says that "such determination of Taiwan's defense needs shall include review by United States military authorities in connection with recommendations to the President and the Congress." In a crisis, Section 3(c) of the TRA requires the President to inform Congress "promptly" of any threat to "the security or the social or economic system" of the people on Taiwan and any danger to U.S. interests. The TRA set up the American Institute in Taiwan (AIT), which continued the functions of the embassy in Taipei. AIT implements policy as directed by the Departments of Defense and State, and the National Security Council (NSC) of the White House. They have controlled notifications to Congress of pending major arms sales, as required by the Arms Export Control Act (AECA), P.L. 90-629.

Congress also oversees the President's implementation of policies decided in 1982. President Ronald Reagan agreed with the PRC on the August 17, 1982, Joint Communique on reducing arms sales to Taiwan, but he also clarified that arms sales would continue in accordance with the TRA and with the full expectation of a peaceful resolution of the Taiwan question. At the same time, Reagan extended "Six Assurances" to Taipei, including assurances that Washington had not agreed to set a date for ending arms sales to Taiwan nor to consult with Beijing on arms sales. (On policy for a peaceful resolution, see CRS Report RL30341, *China/Taiwan: Evolution of the "One China" Policy—Key Statements from Washington, Beijing, and Taipei*, by Shirley A. Kan.)

## Broad Indicators of Arms Transfers

U.S. arms transfers to Taiwan have been significant despite the absence of a defense treaty or a diplomatic relationship. Taiwan has ranked among the top recipients of U.S. arms sales. The value of *deliveries* of *U.S.* defense articles and services to Taiwan totaled $4.1 billion in the 2003-2006 period and $3.0 billion in 2007-2010. Among customers worldwide, Taiwan ranked 4th (behind Egypt, Israel, and Saudi Arabia) in 2003-2006 and 4th (behind Saudi Arabia, Israel, and Egypt) in

2007-2010. In 2010 alone, Taiwan ranked 4th among worldwide recipients, receiving $660 million worth of U.S. defense articles and services. As for *agreements* in 2010 alone, Taiwan ranked 1st as the top customer worldwide, with agreements worth $2.7 billion. Broad values for U.S. arms agreements with and deliveries to Taiwan are summarized below.[1]

| | 2003-2006 period | 2007-2010 period | 2010 |
|---|---|---|---|
| U.S. Agreements | $0.9 billion | $6.6 billion | $2.7 billion |
| U.S. Deliveries | $4.1 billion | $3.0 billion | $0.7 billion |

# Military Relationship

## "Software Initiative"

In addition to transfers of hardware, beginning after the crisis in the Taiwan Strait in 1995-1996 during which President Clinton deployed two aircraft carrier battle groups near Taiwan in March 1996, the Pentagon quietly expanded the sensitive military relationship with Taiwan to levels unprecedented since 1979.[2] The broader exchanges have increased attention to "software," including discussions over strategy, training, logistics, command and control, etc.

Also, Taiwan's F-16 fighter pilots have trained at Luke Air Force Base, AZ, since 1997. However, in 2004, Taiwan's Minister of Defense Lee Jye surprisingly wanted to withdraw the pilots and fighters.[3] In response, the Defense Department stressed the value of continuing the training program to develop "mission ready and experienced pilots" with improved tactical proficiency shown by graduated pilots who have "performed brilliantly," as explicitly notified to Congress.[4]

In July 2001, after U.S. and Taiwan media reported on the "Monterey Talks," a U.S.-Taiwan meeting on national security that was launched in Monterey, CA, the Pentagon revealed it was the seventh meeting (since 1997) held with Taiwan's national security officials "to discuss issues of interaction and means by which to provide for the defense of Taiwan."[5] Another round of such strategic talks took place in July 2002.[6] The 11th round of the talks took place in late September 2005, after the Bush Administration postponed the meeting by a couple of weeks to accommodate PRC ruler Hu Jintao's scheduled visit to Washington on September 7 (which was then postponed because of President Bush's response to Hurricane Katrina).[7] These talks have continued.

Increased U.S. concerns about Taiwan's self-defense capability prompted expanded communication on defense and security matters. At a conference on Taiwan's defense in March 2002, Deputy Secretary of Defense Paul Wolfowitz said that the United States wanted to help

---

[1] CRS Report R42121, *U.S. Arms Sales: Agreements with and Deliveries to Major Clients, 2003-2010*, by Richard F. Grimmett; compiled with U.S. official data as reported by the Defense Security Cooperation Agency (DSCA).

[2] Mann, Jim, "U.S. Has Secretly Expanded Military Ties with Taiwan," *LA Times*, July 24, 1999; Kurt M. Campbell (former Deputy Assistant Secretary of Defense for Asian and Pacific Affairs) and Derek J. Mitchell, "Crisis in the Taiwan Strait?," *Foreign Affairs*, July/August 2001.

[3] *Jane's Defense Weekly*, October 9, 2004, and June 29, 2005; and author's consultations.

[4] DSCA, notification to Congress, October 25, 2005 (see list at end of this CRS Report).

[5] *China Times*, Taipei, July 18, 2001; *Washington Times*, July 18, 2001; Defense Department briefing, July 19, 2001.

[6] *Central News Agency*, Taipei, July 17, 2002.

[7] Project for a New American Century, August 26, 2005; *Taipei Times*, September 15, 2005.

Taiwan's military to strengthen civilian control, enhance jointness, and rationalize arms acquisitions.[8] At a congressional hearing in April 2004, Assistant Secretary of Defense for International Security Affairs Peter Rodman testified that the Pentagon believed Taiwan's military needed to improve readiness, planning, and interoperability among its services.[9]

## Assessments of Taiwan's Defense

The Pentagon has conducted its own assessments of Taiwan's defense needs, with over a dozen studies from 1997 to early 2004.[10] Congress could inquire about these assessments and any other reports. In September 1999, to enhance cooperation, a Pentagon team was said to have visited Taiwan to assess its air defense capability.[11] The Pentagon reportedly completed its classified assessment in January 2000, finding a number of problems in the Taiwan military's ability to defend against aircraft, ballistic missiles, and cruise missiles, and those problems included international isolation, inadequate security, and sharp inter-service rivalries.[12] In September 2000, the Pentagon reportedly conducted a classified assessment of Taiwan's naval defense needs—as the Clinton Administration had promised in April 2000 while deferring a sale of Aegis-equipped destroyers. The report, "Taiwan Naval Modernization," was said to have found that Taiwan's navy needed the Aegis radar system, Kidd-class destroyers, submarines, an anti-submarine underwater sonar array, and P-3 anti-submarine aircraft.[13] On December 18, 2000, the Defense Department issued a "Report to Congress on Implementation of the TRA," in response to the reporting requirement in the Consolidated Appropriations Act for FY2000 (P.L. 106-113).

In January 2001, a Pentagon team reportedly examined Taiwan's command and control, air force equipment, and air defense against a first strike.[14] In September 2001, a Defense Department team reportedly visited Taiwan to assess its army, as the Bush Administration promised in the April 2001 round of arms sales talks.[15] In August 2002, a U.S. military team studied Taiwan's Po Sheng command and control program.[16] In November 2002, another U.S. team visited Taiwan to assess its Marine Corps and security at ports and harbors, and reported positive findings.[17] In November 2003, a U.S. defense team visited Taiwan to assess its anti-submarine warfare (ASW) capability and rated it as poor.[18]

In 2007-2009, Taiwan's Defense Ministry conducted a Joint Defense Capabilities Assessment (JDCA) with U.S. assistance, to determine requirements for Taiwan's joint self-defense.[19] In

---

[8] Deputy Secretary of Defense Paul Wolfowitz, "Remarks to the U.S.-Taiwan Business Council," March 11, 2002.

[9] House International Relations Committee, "The Taiwan Relations Act: The Next 25 Years," April 21, 2004.

[10] Statement of Assistant Secretary of Defense for International Security Affairs Peter Rodman at a hearing on "The Taiwan Relations Act: The Next 25 Years" held by the House International Relations Committee on April 21, 2004.

[11] "U.S. Military Team Arrives in Taiwan for Visit," *Lien-ho Pao [United Daily News]*, September 19, 1999, in *FBIS*.

[12] Ricks, Thomas, "Taiwan Seen as Vulnerable to Attack," *Washington Post*, March 31, 2000.

[13] Tsao, Nadia, "Pentagon Report Says Taiwan Can Handle AEGIS," *Taipei Times*, September 27, 2000; Michael Gordon, "Secret U.S. Study Concludes Taiwan Needs New Arms," *New York Times*, April 1, 2001.

[14] *China Times* (Taiwan), January 14, 2001; *Taipei Times*, January 15, 2001.

[15] *Taipei Times* (Taiwan), September 10, 2001.

[16] *Taiwan Defense Review* (Taiwan), August 27, 2002.

[17] *Taipei Times*, November 21, 2002; January 1, 2003; August 22, 2003; and *Tzu-Yu Shih-Pao*, April 14, 2003.

[18] *Jane's Defense Weekly (JDW)*, December 3, 2003; *Taiwan Defense Review*, January 12, 2004; *JDW*, June 30, 2004.

[19] Fu Mei, briefing at the U.S.-Taiwan Defense Industry Conference, September 29, 2008; and "Defense and Security Report," U.S.-Taiwan Business Council, Annual Review 2009.

---

2010, the Defense Department reportedly began more detailed studies of Taiwan's joint defense transformation.[20]

In 2009, Congress directed the Defense Secretary to assess Taiwan's air defense forces, including its F-16 fighters, with an unclassified report due by January 26, 2010. As directed by the conference report for the National Defense Authorization Act (NDAA) for FY2010 (P.L. 111-84), on February 16, 2010, the Defense Department submitted an unclassified assessment to Congress, concluding that the PLA's ballistic and cruise missiles as well as fighters have diminished Taiwan's ability to deny the PLA air superiority in a conflict.[21] The study found that although Taiwan had almost 400 combat aircraft, far fewer were operationally capable. Taiwan's F-5 fighters already reached the end of their operational service life. Taiwan's Indigenous Defense Fighters (IDFs) lacked the capability for sustained sorties. Taiwan's Mirage-2000 fighters (from France) were technologically advanced but required frequent, expensive maintenance that reduced their readiness rate. The assessment noted that Taiwan recognized its need for sustainable replacements for obsolete and problematic aircraft. This study raised a question of what basis the Bush and Obama Administrations had for not accepting or agreeing to Taiwan's request for new F-16s for almost four years, before there was this assessment. The study also did not address the role of Taiwan's military in deterrence in peacetime. The Congressional directive was a catalyst in advancing the Pentagon's consideration of Taiwan's requirements for air defense. Over one year later, on September 22, 2011, the Defense Department submitted a comprehensive, classified assessment of Taiwan's air power.[22] The Departments of Defense and State briefed the study to committees in the Senate on September 28 and in the House on October 5.

Overall, the Defense Secretary has told Congress in required annual reports (latest in August 2011) on PRC military power that the balance of forces across the Taiwan Strait has continued to shift to the PRC's favor. Moreover, in spite of the closer cross-strait engagement after the KMT's Ma Ying-jeou became President in Taipei in May 2008, the PLA's build-up opposite Taiwan has continued, and "the deployment of advanced capabilities opposite the island have not eased."[23] More specifically, the report noted in 2002 that PRC control over Taiwan would allow the PLA to move its defensive perimeter further out to sea. Also, the Secretary's report on PRC military power had told Congress in March 2009 that it was no longer the case that Taiwan's Air Force enjoyed dominance of the airspace over the strait. In assessing the shifting security situation, Assistant Secretary of Defense for Asian and Pacific Security Affairs Wallace "Chip" Gregson stressed in September 2009 that Taiwan's military will never again have quantitative advantages over the PLA. As a retired lieutenant general of the U.S. Marine Corps, former commander of Marine Corps Forces Pacific, and a combat veteran of the Vietnam War, Gregson appreciated any advantages in defense of an island or a smaller force, and urged Taiwan to shift to stress qualitative advantages, including innovation and asymmetry.[24] This new U.S. stress spurred talks with Taiwan about asymmetrical advantages, with potential implications for arms sales. On

---

[20] *Central News Agency*, October 6, 2010, citing Rupert Hammond-Chambers of the U.S-Taiwan Business Council.

[21] Defense Intelligence Agency, "Taiwan Air Defense Status Assessment," DIA-02-1001-028, dated January 21, 2010.

[22] For media reports: *Washington Times*, September 19, 2011; and Jason Sherman, "Pentagon Provides Congress Secret Report on Taiwan's Air Defense Capabilities," *Inside Defense*, September 27, 2011.

[23] Secretary of Defense, "Military and Security Developments Involving the People's Republic of China, 2011," August 24, 2011. The National Defense Authorization Act for FY2010, P.L. 111-84, changed the title of the annual report from the previous "Military Power of the People's Republic of China."

[24] Wallace Gregson, "Remarks to the U.S.-Taiwan Business Council's Defense Industry Conference," September 28, 2009. On October 4, 2010, Gregson again spoke at the annual conference, in Cambridge, MD, and reiterated the stress on Taiwan's need for innovation and asymmetry. But the Obama Administration did not release his speech.

September 19, 2011, Acting Assistant Secretary of Defense for Asian and Pacific Affairs Peter Lavoy continued to urge Taiwan to stress survivable, credible deterrence and new innovative, asymmetric advantages. While Taiwan's press reported that visiting Deputy Defense Minister Andrew Yang spoke of non-conventional asymmetrical strategies, he did not in his speech.[25]

## Normalized Relationship

The George W. Bush Administration continued the Clinton Administration's initiative and expanded the closer military ties at different levels. In April 2001, President Bush announced he would drop the 20-year-old annual arms talks process used to discuss arms sales to Taiwan's military in favor of normal, routine considerations of Taiwan's requests on an as-needed basis—similar to interactions with other foreign governments.[26]

U.S. military officers observed Taiwan's Hankuang-17 annual military exercise in 2001, the first time since 1979.[27] The Pacific Command (PACOM)'s Asia-Pacific Center for Security Studies (APCSS) accepted fellows from Taiwan in its Executive Course for the first time in the summer of 2002.[28] By the summer of 2002, the U.S. and Taiwan militaries reportedly discussed setting up an undersea ASW link to monitor the PLA Navy's submarines.[29] The U.S. and Taiwan militaries set up a hotline in 2002 to deal with possible crises.[30]

In addition, in 2002, the Administration asked Congress to pass legislation to authorize the assignment of personnel from U.S. departments (including the Defense Department) to AIT, allowing the assignment of active-duty military personnel to Taiwan for the first time since 1979. The objective was to select from a wider range of personnel, without excluding those on active duty. The first active-duty defense attaché since 1979, an Army Colonel began his duty in Taipei in August 2005 with civilian clothes and a status similar to military attaches assigned to Hong Kong, except that military personnel in Hong Kong may wear uniforms at some occasions.[31]

Also, the Acting Under Secretary of Defense for Acquisition, Technology, and Logistics, Michael Wynne, submitted a letter to Congress on August 29, 2003, that designated Taiwan as a "major non-NATO ally."

---

[25] U.S.-Taiwan Business Council, defense industry conference, Richmond, VA, September 18-20, 2011. For the second year, the Obama Administration refused to release the Defense Department's speech, and for the first time, no senior State Department official attended.

[26] On the annual arms talks, see CRS Report RS20365, *Taiwan: Annual Arms Sales Process*, by Shirley A. Kan.

[27] *Chung-Kuo Shih-Pao*, Taipei, July 18, 2001. *China Times* (May 27, 2004) quoted Defense Minister Lee Jye as confirming that U.S. military personnel observed the Hankuang-17, Hankuang-18, and Hankuang-19 exercises.

[28] *CNN.com*, March 18, 2002; Author's discussions in Hawaii in July 2002.

[29] *Tzu-Yu Shih-Pao* [Liberty Times], Taipei, July 20, 2002.

[30] *Jane's Defense Weekly*, October 29, 2003.

[31] In addition to Colonel Al Willner, the Defense Security Cooperation Agency (DSCA) assigned Army Colonel Peter Notarianni to oversee security assistance programs at AIT in Taipei. Department of Defense, notice, "DSCA contract awarded to AIT to support DSCA active-duty military and civil service personnel," September 24, 2005. In the past, from 1951 to 1979, the United States assigned to Taiwan the Military Assistance Advisory Group (MAAG). (See Ministry of National Defense, *U.S. MAAG – Taiwan: an Oral History*, Taipei: 2008. One of the officers interviewed was retired Colonel Mason Young, Jr., father of Stephen Young who served as AIT Director from 2006 to 2009.)

## Senior-Level Exchanges, Exercises, Crisis Management

The United States and Taiwan have held high-level defense-related meetings in the United States. The Bush Administration granted a visa for Defense Minister Tang Yiau-ming to visit the United States to attend an industry conference held by the U.S.-Taiwan Business Council on March 10-12, 2002 (in St. Petersburg, FL), making him the first ROC defense minister to come to the United States on a nontransit purpose since 1979.[32] Tang met with Deputy Secretary of Defense Paul Wolfowitz at the conference.[33]

However, after that policy change in 2002, Taiwan's defense minister declined to visit the United States through 2007. In September 2002, a deputy defense minister, Kang Ning-hsiang, visited Washington and was the first senior Taiwan defense official to have meetings inside the Pentagon since U.S.-ROC diplomatic ties severed in 1979, although a meeting with Wolfowitz took place outside the Pentagon.[34] In January 2003, a Taiwanese newspaper leaked information that a U.S. military team planned to participate in—beyond observe—the Hankuang-19 military exercise and be present at Taiwan's Hengshan Command Center for the first time since 1979.[35] On the same day, General Chen Chao-min, a deputy defense minister, confirmed to Taiwan's legislature a U.S. plan for a noncombatant evacuation operation (NEO). However, the leak and confirmation reportedly prompted annoyance in Washington and contributed to a U.S. decision to limit General Chen's visit to the United States in February 2003 to attendance at a private sector conference on Taiwan's defense (in San Antonio, TX), without a visit to Washington.[36] Deputy Assistant Secretary of Defense Richard Lawless and Deputy Assistant Secretary of State Randall Schriver met with General Chen. In October 2004, Taiwan's Deputy Minister for Armaments, General Huoh Shoou-yeh, attended a U.S.-Taiwan defense industry conference (in Scottsdale, AZ), instead of Defense Minister Lee Jye.

In May 2005, the Chief of General Staff, General Lee Tien-yu, visited the United States, but he was the first Chief of General Staff from Taiwan willing to make the biennial visit since General Tang Fei's visit in 1998.[37] In September 2005, Deputy Minister Huoh again attended a U.S.-Taiwan defense industry conference (in San Diego, CA). Deputy Defense Minister Ko Chen-heng attended the next conference in September 2006 (in Denver, CO). In July 2007, Chief of General Staff, General Huoh Shoou-yeh, visited the United States.[38] At the defense industry conference in September 2007 (in Annapolis, MD), Deputy Minister Ko again represented Taiwan, as Defense Minister Lee Tien-yu declined to visit the United States. In only the second visit by a defense minister from Taiwan since 1979, Minister Chen Chao-min visited the United States on September 28–October 5, 2008, attending the U.S.-Taiwan Defense Industry Conference in Jacksonville, FL, and visiting Luke Air Force Base, Naval Warfare Systems Command in San Diego, and the Pacific Command in Honolulu.[39] In June 2009, Chief of General Staff, Admiral Lin Jan-yi, visited the United States.[40] However, Defense Minister Kao Hua-chu declined to visit

---

[32] In December 2001, Defense Minister Wu Shih-wen made a U.S. transit on his way to the Dominican Republic.

[33] Deputy Secretary of Defense Paul Wolfowitz, "Remarks to the U.S.-Taiwan Business Council," March 11, 2002.

[34] *Reuters*, September 10, 2002.

[35] *Chung-Kuo Shih-Pao [China Times]*, January 2, 2003.

[36] *Taiwan Defense Review*, January 18, 2003; *Straits Times* (Singapore), January 21, 2003.

[37] *Lien-Ho Pao [United Daily News]* (Taipei), May 26, 2005.

[38] *China Times*, Taipei, July 13, 2007.

[39] Speech by Deputy Assistant Secretary of Defense David Sedney, in Jacksonville, FL, September 29, 2008.

[40] *Tzu-yu Shih-pao [Liberty Times]*, Taipei, June 19, 2009.

for the annual defense conferences in 2009, 2010, and 2011. Instead, deputy ministers of defense represented Taiwan in talks with senior U.S. officials and private industry executives.

As mentioned above, U.S. military observation of Taiwan's Hankuang military exercises resumed in 2001. The Hankuang-19 exercise took place in April-May 2003, with participation by about 20 U.S. military personnel and retired Admiral Dennis Blair, who just resigned as the Commander of the Pacific Command (PACOM). (Blair led U.S. observers through the Hankuang-24 exercise in June 2008. In 2009, he became the Director of National Intelligence (DNI).) The 2003 exercise reportedly raised questions about the military's will to fight and ability to sustain defense before possible U.S. support.[41] Deputy Defense Minister Lin Chong-pin visited Washington in June 2003 to respond to concerns about Taiwan's commitment to self-defense. The Hankuang-20 exercise reportedly included a U.S.-provided computer simulation in August 2004 that resulted in the PLA invading and capturing the capital, Taipei, within six days.[42] In April 2006, Taiwan's President Chen Shui-bian and other officials held a Yushan exercise to improve crisis-management and continuity-of-government to counter any PLA "decapitation" attack, with no U.S. participation.[43] Then, in April 2008, AIT Director Stephen Young and other U.S. officials observed the Yushan exercise for the first time, but some KMT politicians criticized the inclusion of U.S. observers.

The KMT's Ma Ying-jeou became president in May 2008. In December 2008, Defense Minister Chen Chao-min announced a reduction in the frequency of the Hankuang live-fire field exercises to change them from annual to biennial exercises (only once in two years), raising questions about training, readiness, as well as contacts with the U.S. military. Hankuang-25 was held in June 2009. Retired Admiral Robert Natter (former Commander of the Navy's Atlantic Fleet) led U.S. military observers to the exercise. Meanwhile, President Ma renamed the crisis-management exercise from Yushan to Chunghsing, changed the scenario from a PLA attack to domestic disasters, and did not invite U.S. officials to observe like in 2008.[44]

However, two months later, President Ma and his officials faced difficulties in managing relief for the disaster caused by Typhoon Morakot that hit Taiwan on August 8, 2009. With hundreds of people buried in a landslide, Taiwan's government initially declined to request foreign aid and did not ask for American assistance until August 13. On August 16 and 17, the U.S. military provided assistance with the arrival in Taiwan of two KC-130 transport aircraft from Okinawa, Japan, as well as the *USS Denver* (the Navy's amphibious transport dock based in Sasebo, Japan) with two MH-53 and two MH-60 Marine Corps heavy-lift helicopters in disaster relief operations. (The U.S. military previously had supported disaster relief in Taiwan after the earthquake on September 21, 1999, and the Typhoon Aere in 2004.) In his national day address on October 10, 2009, President Ma recognized mainland China for its aid that "exceeded those of all other nations," without mentioning the United States in his speech.

---

[41] *Lien-Ho Pao [United Daily News]* (Taipei), April 16, 2003; *China Times* (Taipei), April 19, 2003; *Taipei Times*, April 25, 2003; *Central News Agency* (Taipei), May 9, 2003.

[42] *AFP*, August 11, 2004; *Taiwan News*, August 12, 2004.

[43] *Liberty Times* (Taipei), April 13 and 16, 2006; and author's interviews in Taipei.

[44] York Chen (was in Chen Shui-bian's NSC), "Exercises Give Chance to Test Mettle," *Taipei Times*, March 31, 2009; U.S.-Taiwan Business Council, "Defense & Security Report," First Quarter, 2009.

# April 2001 Arms Requests and Status of Arms Sales

## April 2001 Decisions

In 2001, arms sales talks took place on April 24 in Washington, DC, and Taiwan was represented by its Vice Chief of General Staff, General Huoh Shou-yeh. According to the Administration and news reports,[45] President Bush *approved* Taiwan's request for: 8 diesel-electric submarines; 12 P-3C Orion anti-submarine warfare (ASW) aircraft (linked to the submarine sale); 54 Mark-48 ASW torpedoes; 44 Harpoon submarine-launched anti-ship cruise missiles; 144 M109A6 Paladin self-propelled howitzers; 54 AAV7A1 amphibious assault vehicles; AN/ALE-50 electronic countermeasure (ECM) systems for F-16s; and 12 MH-53 mine-sweeping helicopters. President Bush approved four decommissioned Kidd-class destroyers for sale as Excess Defense Articles (EDA). Bush also decided to brief Taiwan's military on the PAC-3 missile defense missile.[46]

President Bush *deferred* decisions on destroyers equipped with the Aegis combat system. Bush also deferred decisions on M1A2 Abrams main battle tanks and AH-64D Apache Longbow attack helicopters, pending a U.S. assessment of Taiwan's army. (The United States later approved Taiwan's request for Abrams tanks in 2001. Also, in the fall of 2008, the U.S. Army briefed Taiwan's army on the M1A2 tank and an upgraded M8 armored gun system. By early 2009, Taiwan's army estimated the total cost of under 150 new tanks at about US$2.9 billion.[47])

President Bush *denied* Taiwan's requests for Joint Direct Attack Munitions (JDAM) and High-speed Anti-radiation Missiles (HARM) that target radar-equipped air defense systems. At the U.S.-Taiwan Business Council's conference in February 2003, however, Deputy Under Secretary of the Air Force Willard Mitchell indicated that these requests were under review. A possible basis for reviewing any renewed requests from Taiwan was found in the Pentagon's report on PRC Military Power submitted in July 2003 to Congress, which confirmed that the PLA procured from Israel "a significant number of HARPY anti-radiation systems." The press first reported on the PLA's acquisition of the HARPY attack drones in 2002.[48] By the second half of 2004, the Administration reportedly considered Taiwan's new request for the HARM (submitted in August 2004), while a decision on JDAM guidance kits also remained pending.[49] However, in 2005, the Bush Administration reportedly denied these requests.[50] Yet, in September 2011, the Obama Administration notified Congress of upgrades to Taiwan's F-16A/B fighters, including JDAMs.

---

[45] White House, press briefing, April 24, 2001; Department of Defense, news briefing, April 24, 2001;David Sanger, "Bush is Offering Taiwanese Some Arms, But Not the Best," *New York Times*, April 24, 2001; Steven Mufson and Dana Milbank, "Taiwan to Get Variety of Arms," *Washington Post*, April 24, 2001; Neil King Jr., "Bush Defers Sale of Aegis to Taiwan, Will Offer Four Kidd-Class Destroyers," *Wall Street Journal*, April 24, 2001; "U.S. Refuses Taiwan Request for JDAM, HARM, and PAC-3 Missiles," *Aerospace Daily*, April 25, 2001; and "U.S. Formally Informs ROC of Arms Sales Decision," *Central News Agency* (Taiwan), April 25, 2001.

[46] *Taiwan Defense Review*, January 18, 2003, reported the briefing took place in late 2001.

[47] Mark Stokes, "Taiwan's Security: Beyond the Special Budget," AEI, March 27, 2006; U.S.-Taiwan Business Council, "Defense & Security Report," Second Quarter 2009.

[48] *Washington Times*, July 2, 2002; *Guangzhou Daily* (via FBIS), July 4, 2002; *Ha'aretz*, Tel Aviv, July 25, 2002; *Flight International*, November 5-11, 2002.

[49] *Taiwan News*, October 6, 2004; *Washington Times*, October 8, 2004; *Taiwan Defense Review*, November 26, 2004.

[50] Wendell Minnick, "U.S. Rejects Taiwan Request for HARM and JDAM Kits," *Jane's Defense Weekly*, January 18, 2006.

---

## Taiwan's Decisions

After the U.S. response to Taiwan's requests in 2001, attention turned to Taiwan, where the military, civilian officials, and competing political parties in a newly assertive legislature (Legislative Yuan, or LY) have debated contentious issues. These issues include the urgency of a possible PLA attack, how much to spend on defense, which U.S. weapons systems to buy, whether to respond to perceived U.S. pressure, and what the defense strategy should be. The debate has taken place as the Pentagon has warned of the PLA's accelerated buildup in a coercive strategy targeting Taiwan. In early 2003, the Bush Administration stressed to Taiwan the imperatives of missile defense, command and control, and anti-submarine warfare (ASW). In March 2003, Taiwan's Defense Ministry issued a new procurement plan emphasizing those priorities.[51] However, setting priorities, forging a national consensus, and funding defense programs have remained contentious in Taiwan's politicized debate over national security.

## Amphibious Assault Vehicles

Taiwan agreed to purchase the AAV7A1 amphibious assault vehicles, under a program managed by the U.S. Marine Corps. The Bush Administration notified Congress in September 2002. United Defense Industries obtained a contract in June 2003, and deliveries began in March 2005.[52] Taiwan could request additional AAV7A1s.

## Attack and Utility Helicopters

After deferring a decision on Taiwan's request for attack helicopters, the Bush Administration, in May 2002, approved the request, and Taiwan began negotiations on 30 AH-64D Apache Longbow helicopters sold by Boeing.[53] Afterwards, Taiwan also considered the AH-1Z Cobra helicopters sold by Bell.[54] In April 2007, Taiwan's military decided to procure 30 Apaches.[55] Also, in 2005, Taiwan requested price and availability data for acquisition of 60 utility helicopters.[56] In 2005, Bell proposed its UH-1Y Huey utility helicopter, and Sikorsky proposed its UH-60 Black Hawk helicopters as replacement for Taiwan's UH-1H Huey utility helicopters. In the LY in December 2007, inter-party negotiations and the final decision approved about $203 million but froze two-thirds, or $135 million, for 60 UH-60M Black Hawk utility helicopters. Also in the 2008 defense budget, the LY approved $228 million for 30 Apache helicopters.

On October 3, 2008, President Bush finally notified Congress of the proposed Foreign Military Sale (FMS) program of 30 Apache helicopters for a total value of $2.532 billion. However, in what observers noted was an apparent arbitrary decision, the President did not notify Congress of the pending sale of Black Hawk utility helicopters, which required notification at a later time. Taiwan signed a Letter of Offer and Acceptance for the Apaches in 2009.[57]

---

[51] *Taiwan Defense Review*, March 12, 2003.

[52] *Jane's International Defense Review*, September 2003; *Taiwan Defense Review*, March 4, 2005.

[53] *Taipei Times*, May 26, 2002; *Jane's Defense Weekly*, June 5, 2002.

[54] *Jane's Defense Weekly*, March 10 and 24, 2004.

[55] *AFP*, April 12, 2007; *Lien-Ho Pao*, July 9, 2007; *Defense News*, July 16, 2007.

[56] *Jane's Defense Weekly*, August 24, 2005; *Defense News*, July 16, 2007.

[57] *Defense News*, April 12, 2010.

Taiwan's 2009 defense budget included about $230 million for the program to procure 60 Black Hawk helicopters.[58] However, after Typhoon Morakot battered Taiwan on August 8-10, 2009, President Ma responded to domestic criticism of his crisis-management and disaster relief in part by announcing on August 18 that he would cut the purchase from 60 to 45 Black Hawks and use what he claimed would be $300 million in so-called "savings" to purchase strictly civilian rescue helicopters. However, that contradictory decision also called for the military to beef up its role in disaster relief, which would require more helicopters like the Black Hawks. The military's helicopters already have served dual (military and civilian) missions. President Ma apparently did not consult with the Defense Ministry, which announced on August 30 that it would preserve the pending program to procure 60 Black Hawk helicopters, to avoid delays and costly changes in procurement process, and to maintain the objective of upgrading combat readiness. The Defense Ministry already had prepared and submitted a Letter of Request for U.S. consideration. While agreeing, Ma nonetheless directed the Defense Ministry to work on diverting 15 of the new military helicopters to the Interior Ministry, which would detract from national defense. Meanwhile, the military already considered options to increase its assistance to disaster relief, which would require more (not less) helicopters that serve dual (military or civilian) tasks, while upgrading combat capabilities in acquiring the 60 Black Hawks. The Defense Ministry also had concerns that the Interior Ministry lacked the capability to maintain and operate the helicopters or train pilots, which could increase the burden on the military. Finally, on January 29, 2010, President Obama notified Congress of a sale of the helicopters for $3.1 billion.

## Kidd-Class Destroyers

In October 2002, the Defense Committee of Taiwan's legislature engaged in a sharp partisan debate over whether to approve funding (about $800 million) to buy the U.S. Navy's four available Kidd-class destroyers, ending with 18 lawmakers from the ruling Democratic Progressive Party (DPP) and Taiwan Solidarity Union (TSU) voting in favor, against 16 legislators from the opposition Kuomintang (KMT) and People's First Party (PFP).[59] In November 2002, the Bush Administration notified Congress of the proposed sale of four Kidd-class destroyers for about $875 million. Then, on May 30, 2003, Taiwan's legislature finally voted to release the funding, after they conditioned funding on bargaining with the U.S. Navy on a 15% price reduction. The U.S. Navy began reactivation and upgrade of the Kidds in July 2003[60] for delivery of the 9,600-ton destroyers ahead of schedule from October 2005 to 2006. Taiwan's Naval Commander-in-Chief, Marine General Chen Pang-chih, attended the transfer ceremony in Charleston, SC, for the first two destroyers on October 29, 2005, in the presence of Representative Henry Brown. The destroyers, the largest warships in Taiwan's navy, arc equipped with SM-2 air-defense missiles and a joint combat management system. The transfer ceremony for the final two Kidds took place in Charleston, SC, on August 25, 2006. After the transfer of the Kidds, a follow-on issue has been whether Taiwan would acquire more SM-2 missiles.

---

[58] Max Hirsch, "U.S. to Approve Major Helicopter Sale to Taiwan This Year," *Kyodo*, March 9, 2009.

[59] Author's visit to Taiwan; and *Taipei Times* and *China Post* (Taipei), November 1, 2002.

[60] *Taipei Times*, September 5, 2003; *Taiwan Defense Review*, March 10, 2004; *Taipei Times*, September 15, 2004; *Jane's Defense Weekly*, November 10, 2004.

## Aegis-Equipped Destroyers

The Department of Defense considered the Kidds as platforms to provide Taiwan's navy with the necessary operational experience before any possible acquisition of more advanced Aegis-equipped ships.[61] The U.S. Navy deploys the Aegis combat system (e.g., on the Arleigh Burke-class destroyer) for air defense and applies it in development of a future Navy missile defense system (using SM-3 missiles). An alternative to the Arleigh Burke that retains the Aegis Spy-1D radar, called the Evolved Advanced Combat System (EACS) has been considered. The Aegis combat system has the capability to track over 100 targets and to conduct simultaneous anti-air, anti-surface, and anti-submarine operations. During the U.S. war in Iraq in 2003, the Aegis combat system helped the Patriot missile defense system to detect and intercept Iraqi missiles.[62] In 2002, Taiwan again requested four Arleigh Burke-class, Aegis-equipped destroyers, for delivery in 2010 and at a cost of about $4.8 billion. Taiwan did not get a U.S. response.[63]

## Submarines

Despite initial skepticism about the Bush Administration's April 2001 agreement to sell Taiwan submarines (since the United States no longer manufactures diesel-electric submarines), the Department of Defense has discussed options for a Foreign Military Sales (FMS) program for eight boats with U.S. and foreign companies and Taiwan. In addition to the military and political implications of selling submarines to Taiwan's navy, issues for Congress include potential technology transfers to Taiwan and European countries, and leaks of secrets from Taiwan to the PRC, that could involve U.S. submarine secrets and implications for the U.S. military.[64] In a report to Congress, as required by the National Defense Authorization Act for FY1992-FY1993, the Secretary of the Navy reported in May 1992 that "to the extent that a potential diesel submarine construction project would draw on U.S. resources, it has the potential to tap into the state-of-the-art technology used in U.S. nuclear powered submarines." The report also noted "the fact that the diesel submarine is not a viable asset in the U.S. Navy" and that "construction of diesel submarines for export in U.S. shipyards would not support the U.S. submarine shipbuilding base and could encourage future development and operation of diesel submarines to the detriment of our own forces." The report also said that "it may be possible to control the release of the most important information and specific technologies of concern, but an effective system would also have significant costs. The problem will be more difficult, however, if a foreign entity is present in the shipyards during submarine construction."

In November 2001, seven companies submitted bids and concept papers to the Department of the Navy. Companies interested in the contract reportedly include U.S. manufacturers, Northrop Grumman (with its Ingalls Shipbuilding shipyard) and General Dynamics (with its Electric Boat shipyard); Germany's HDW; the Netherlands' RDM (which sold its Zwaardvis-class submarine design to Taiwan in the 1980s for two Hai Lung [Sea Dragon]-class submarines); France's DCN; and Spain's IZAR (now Navantia). Although the Administration promised to help Taiwan buy submarines, not build them, Taiwan's China Shipbuilding Corporation also became interested in a

---

[61] Consultations; and Wendell Minnick, "What Those Systems are All About," *Topics*, November 2004.

[62] Discussion with Lockheed Martin executive, June 10, 2004; and U.S. Army, 32nd Army Air and Missile Defense Command, Fort Bliss, TX, "Operation Iraqi Freedom: Theater Air and Missile Defense," September 2003.

[63] *Lien-Ho Pao*, September 1, 2004; *Taiwan Defense Review*, December 19, 2004; author's consultations.

[64] As for U.S. counter-espionage concerns, the FBI sent agents to Taipei to investigate alleged compromises of security on the PRC's behalf at Taiwan military's Chungshan Institute of Science and Technology (*CNA*, August 13, 2003).

part of the contract, with support from some of Taiwan's legislators. The U.S. Navy discussed options with Taiwan's Navy in July 2002 and initially planned to select the manufacturer(s) to design and build the submarines in the latter half of 2003.[65] On December 6, 2002, Secretary of the Navy Gordon England informed Congress in a Determination and Findings memo that bidding would be limited to four U.S. companies and the diesel subs would be of U.S. origin.[66] The U.S. Navy held a second Industry Day on December 17, 2002, with General Dynamics, Northrop Grumman, Lockheed Martin, and Raytheon interested in being the prime contractor.[67]

The U.S. Navy provided the Independent Cost Estimate (ICE) on January 17, 2003.[68] The ICE put the sub program at about $10.5 billion, but private sector estimates have been said to be lower (perhaps $6-7 billion). Greater risks and costs were factored into the ICE because of uncertainty about funding by Taiwan and the availability of European designs.

However, by April 2003, the sale became at risk, when the United States and Taiwan reached an impasse over the program start-up costs estimated by the U.S. Navy at $333 million, but offered at $28.5 million by Taiwan. On May 20-23, 2003, Taiwan's Navy sent a delegation led by Vice Admiral Kao Yang to Washington to discuss the issue, but the differences reportedly remained unresolved.[69] Facing the delays in Taiwan's commitment of funds (although it first requested submarines in 1995) and a long acquisition process, the Administration then viewed the program as a long-term solution for Taiwan that would not meet the near-term blockade and submarine threats posed by the PLA Navy.[70] Defense Minister Tang Yiau-ming told visiting AIT Chairwoman Therese Shaheen on October 16, 2003, that Taiwan still placed a high priority on acquiring the submarines.[71] Meanwhile, in 2003, the Bush Administration inquired with Italy about buying eight decommissioning Sauro-class diesel-electric submarines for the estimated cost of about $2 billion for delivery starting in 2006, but Taiwan's military opted for new subs.[72]

A team from the U.S. Navy's International Program Office arrived in Taipei in October 2003, for further talks on whether Taiwan will procure submarines.[73] The U.S. team also met with some of Taiwan's legislators, including Lin Yu-fang of the opposition People First Party.[74] Lin was one of the sponsors of legislation passed in May 2002, requiring Taiwan's navy to arrange for six of the eight submarines to be built in Taiwan using technology transfers.[75] The total cost of new submarines was estimated at $9-12 billion,[76] leading Taiwan's political leaders to consider a controversial Special Budget.[77] (See discussion on budgets below.)

---

[65] *Central News Agency* (Taiwan), July 30, 2002; *Taipei Times*, July 31, 2002; *Defense Daily*, September 16, 2002.

[66] Gordon England, Memorandum to Congress with Determination and Findings, December 6, 2002.

[67] *Knight-Ridder/Tribune Business News*, December 17, 2002.

[68] *Tung-sen Hsin-wen Pao*, Taipei, September 28, 2005.

[69] *United Daily News*, April 21, 2003, and April 22, 2003; *Taiwan Defense Review*, May 17, 2003, and May 30, 2003.

[70] U.S.-Taiwan Business Council, *Defense and Aerospace Report*, Second Quarter 2003; *Bloomberg*, July 10, 2003; *Defense Daily*, July 11, 2003; *TDReview*, September 19, 2003.

[71] *Central News Agency*, Taipei, October 16, 2003.

[72] Wendell Minnick, "Submarine Decisions Show Lack of Creativity," *Taipei Times*, October 16, 2004.

[73] *Lien-ho Pao* [United Daily News], Taipei, October 23, 2003; *Central News Agency*, Taipei, October 26, 2003.

[74] *Taipei Times*, October 31, 2003; *Central News Agency*, November 2, 2003.

[75] Author's discussion with Lin Yu-fang in Taipei in December 2003.

[76] *Lien-ho Pao* [United Daily News], August 25, 2003; *Taipei Times*, October 31, 2003.

[77] *Taiwan Defense Review*, April 30, 2004.

Taiwan's new demand for domestic industrial participation had added another issue and greater potential costs to the program (about $2.5 billion to the total), which U.S. Navy officials discussed with potential prime contractors at the third Industry Day meeting on December 15, 2003, in Washington.[78] However, Deputy Secretary of Defense Wolfowitz told Taiwan's visiting legislative delegation on June 21, 2004, that the Bush Administration approved Taiwan's request for assistance in purchasing submarines but was opposed to Taiwan's new proposal to build them in Taiwan.[79] With U.S. opposition to Taiwan's domestic production of submarines conveyed in official letters from the Defense Department in May and July 2004, Minister of Defense Lee Jye estimated that the cost of the submarines could be reduced.[80] Depending on the funds ultimately approved in Taiwan, the scope of a program could be restricted to fewer than eight boats.

Thus, with delays in Taiwan's decision-making after 2001, Taiwan's request for and the Bush Administration's approval of a sale of submarines met with mixed opinions in Taipei and Washington. In early 2003, officials in the Bush Administration stressed ASW surveillance as one priority for Taiwan's military to consider, with the focus on static arrays and patrol aircraft to track submarines. The Administration approved submarines but did not consider them a priority.[81]

In early 2006, articles appeared alleging that the U.S. Navy failed to effectively implement the diesel sub program for Taiwan, in part to protect the nuclear-powered submarine capability.[82] The Defense Department and the Navy repeated that they supported President Bush's 2001 policy decision on arms sales to Taiwan, but that Taiwan must commit to fund the program. In February 2006, Representative Rob Simmons visited Taiwan, saying that he represented his district in Connecticut, home to General Dynamics' Electric Boat shipyard. In a speech at the American Chamber of Commerce in Taipei, Simmons suggested that the subs could cost less, perhaps around $8 billion, and proposed an interim step to break the impasse whereby Taiwan could procure a sub design first, costing perhaps $225 million.[83] The Navy and DSCA said that Taiwan could first submit a request for a sub design phase.[84]

On April 3, 2006, Taiwan's military submitted a request for U.S. assessment of the feasibility of using two phases (design then perhaps construction). Deputy Under Secretary of Defense Richard Lawless conveyed the U.S. policy response to Taiwan's defense minister in an official letter on June 27, 2006, stating that a two-phased approach was "legally permissible and administratively feasible." However, Lawless warned that such a program likely would increase costs and risks, making foreign design firms and their governments less willing to participate. The Defense Department estimated the design phase to cost $360 million, if Taiwan requested it.[85] Following Lawless' letter, Representative Rob Simmons wrote a letter to Defense Minister Lee Jye on July

---

[78] Ibid., February 6, 2004, and April 30, 2004.

[79] *United Daily News* (Taipei), June 23, 2004.

[80] *Lien-Ho Pao*, September 8, 2004; *CNA*, October 19, 2004. Deputy Under Secretary of Defense Richard Lawless referred to his previous letters of May 20 and July 7, 2004, in a letter to Defense Minister Lee Jye on June 27, 2006.

[81] U.S.-Taiwan Business Council, *Defense and Security Report,* 2nd Quarter 2005.

[82] Wendell Minnick, "Taiwan Claims U.S. Navy is Sabotaging SSK Plans," *Jane's Defense Weekly*, February 15, 2006; "Come Clean on Subs," editorial, *Defense News*, February 13, 2006.

[83] News from Rob Simmons, February 17, 2006; Central News Agency, February 22, 2006; *Taipei Times*, February 23, 2006; *Defense News*, February 27, 2006; and AmCham's *Taiwan Business Topics*, March 2006.

[84] Interviews with Navy and DSCA officials, including consultations in Taipei in April 2006.

[85] Letter from Richard Lawless to Taiwan's Defense Minister Lee Jye, June 27, 2006; Jim Wolf, "U.S. Clears Two-Stage Path to Taiwan Submarine Deal," *Reuters*, July 14, 2006.

---

17, noting that the next step was for Taiwan to request a letter of agreement for the first phase of a sub design.[86] In answer to a question posed by Representative Simmons at a meeting of the Congressional Shipbuilding Caucus on September 27, 2006, Deputy Secretary of Defense Gordon England wrote that his department stood ready to support the U.S. effort to help Taiwan acquire submarines, if Taiwan provided the necessary funds.[87]

Meanwhile, the U.S. Navy requested funds from Taiwan to keep an office to manage the sub program and reportedly warned Taiwan in August 2005 that the "pre-selection" process would stop without such funds. Through March 2006, Taiwan paid $7.5 million to retain the office.[88]

On June 15, 2007, Taiwan's legislature passed the 2007 defense budget with $6 million to fund a "feasibility study" (with LY participation) and did not commit to the design phase or full procurement of submarines (the two U.S.-approved options). Representative James Langevin expressed concerns in a letter to the Secretary of Defense and asked for a review of the U.S. proposal to Taiwan.[89] For the study, a LY delegation met with companies and officials in the United States in August 2007. The LY delegation was positive about its visit but did not reach a conclusion about the sub procurement. In September 2007, the stance of the KMT's presidential candidate, Ma Ying-yeou, was to support the sub purchase, but a KMT legislator who was in the LY delegation of August suggested a possible "new list" of arms requests depending on the outcome of the presidential election in March 2008.[90]

Taiwan's Defense Ministry requested in the 2008 defense budget about US$169 million as the first of three annual installments for the design phase (total of US$360 million). The LY's defense committee kept the requested amount in the defense budget that it approved in October 2007, but the question of procurement was left for inter-party negotiations and the full LY to address. In December 2007, the LY approved the 2008 defense budget with the funds for the sub program cut to US$61.5 million. With one-sixth of the required amount, questions arose about Taiwan's full funding for the design phase and how the U.S. Navy would be able to execute the first phase as approved by the Defense Department in June 2006. Nevertheless, in January 2008, Navy Secretary Donald Winter assured Representative Joe Courtney that Taiwan was required to commit to fully fund phase one and incremental payments would be acceptable.[91] Later in January 2008, the Navy accepted Taiwan's Letter of Request (LOR) for the sub design phase.[92] Then, a Navy team visited Taiwan in March 2008 to discuss details of the program.[93]

However, on October 3, 2008, after the KMT's Ma Ying-jeou became president in May, the Bush Administration did not submit for congressional review the pending submarine design program, while notifying Congress of six other proposed arms sales to Taiwan. Representative Courtney wrote to Secretary of State Condoleezza Rice on October 6, 2008, to inquire about the status of

---

[86] Letter from Rob Simmons to Defense Minister Lee Jye, July 17, 2006.

[87] Gordon England, letter to Rob Simmons, October 24, 2006.

[88] *National Journal*, April 6, 2006; and author's interviews in Taipei in April 2006.

[89] James Langevin, letter to Secretary of Defense Robert Gates, July 20, 2007.

[90] Su Chi's remarks at U.S.-Taiwan Business Council, Defense Industry Conference, Annapolis, September 10-11, 2007; author's consultations in Taipei in November 2007.

[91] Assistant Secretary of the Navy John Thackrah, letter of response, January 18, 2008.

[92] Consultations with TECRO, January and February 2008.

[93] Wendell Minnick, "Hurdles Await Taiwan Efforts to Move Forward on Submarines," *Defense News*, March 17, 2008.

the submarine design program given the failure to notify Congress. Reportedly, in 2008, President Ma reevaluated then reaffirmed the program (adjusted with a goal of some local construction, if not development).[94] In his public remarks delivered to the United States on April 22, 2009, President Ma affirmed to the Obama Administration Taiwan's continued commitment to request the sub design program. Also, in late 2009, Taiwan's LY and military remained committed to the procurement of new submarines.[95] However, like President Bush, President Obama did not submit for congressional review the pending program for a submarine design when he notified Congress of five other programs in January 2010. Despite U.S.-Taiwan commitments, the Obama Administration claimed it made no decision to rule in or rule out the submarine program, even though the United States could have given Taiwan a clear answer of denial. Prospects for the sub program appeared to be unlikely as a U.S. FMS program. Taiwan's alternatives included domestic construction and/or commercial contracts, including for small subs. Still, on January 25, 2011, President Ma reiterated to visiting AIT Chairman Ray Burghardt Taiwan's need to buy subs and F-16C/D fighters to replace aging equipment (that could be four boats). Also, Shuai Hua-ming, a key legislator in the LY's Foreign Affairs and National Defense Committee, visited Washington on February 10-11, and reaffirmed Taiwan's need for subs. In an address to the United States on May 12, 2011, President Ma reiterated Taiwan's need to buy F-16C/D fighters and submarines, primarily for leverage in political negotiations with Beijing. Military analysts, like Mark Stokes, have cited submarines for Taiwan's survival, credible deterrence and asymmetrical advantages.

## P-3C ASW Aircraft

After the United States approved Taiwan's request for 12 P-3C planes, the two sides have negotiated the proposed sale. But Taiwan questioned the estimated cost of $300 million per new plane (in part due to Lockheed Martin's need to reopen the production line) for a total cost of $4.1 billion (including parts and training) and sought alternatives in 2003, such as refurbished P-3Bs or surplus P-3Cs retired from the U.S. Navy's fleet. A longer-term option was the Multi-Mission Maritime Aircraft (MMA) under development by Boeing's subsidiary, McDonnell Douglas, for the U.S. Navy. In 2004, Taiwan's Ministry of Defense sought approval from the Legislative Yuan (LY) of a Special Budget to include funds (about $1.6 billion) for 12 refurbished P-3C ASW planes (sold as Excess Defense Articles) with possible delivery in 2008-2011.[96] The sale became more complicated in 2006, when L-3 Communications wanted to compete.[97] The LY committed to the procurement of the P-3C planes by budgeting about $188 million in the 2007 defense budget passed on June 15, 2007 (with a total program cost of $1.4 billion). About three months later in September 2007, the Bush Administration notified Congress of the proposed sale of 12 excess P-3C aircraft (and support) worth $1.96 billion. Upon this notification, China's military showed its displeasure by refusing to carry out U.S.-PLA military exchanges for about a month. In March 2009, Lockheed Martin received the contract to refurbish the P-3Cs by 2015.

---

[94] *Asia-Pacific Defense Magazine*, September 2008; U.S.-Taiwan Business Council, "Defense & Security Report," 1st Quarter 2009.

[95] Author's consultations in Taipei in November 2009.

[96] *Taiwan Defense Review*, April 30, 2004.

[97] *China Times*, Taipei, September 4, 2006; *Jane's Defense Weekly*, October 18, 2006.

## Patriot Missile Defense

After U.S. approval in 1992, Taiwan in 1997 acquired three Patriot missile defense fire units with PAC-2 Guidance Enhanced Missiles. In the late 1990s, Congress also encouraged the Defense Department to stress Taiwan's missile defense capability in a regional context. After the Bush Administration in 2001 decided to brief Taiwan on the advanced PAC-3 hit-to-kill missile, Taiwan considered buying the PAC-3 system. (The U.S. Army completed developmental testing of the PAC-3 in October 2001 and conducted operational tests in 2002. The PAC-3 has been deployed with the U.S. Army, as seen in Operation Iraqi Freedom during March-April 2003. Raytheon describes its Patriot system as the world's most advanced ground-based system for defense against aircraft, theater ballistic missiles, and cruise missiles.)

In late 2002, the Pentagon reportedly was disappointed with Taiwan's delay in requesting the PAC-3 missiles.[98] At a private sector conference on Taiwan's defense in February 2003, Bush Administration officials openly stressed to Taiwan's visiting Deputy Defense Minister Chen Chao-min the imperative of acquiring advanced missile defense systems. In March 2003, Mary Tighe, the Director of Asian and Pacific Affairs, led a Defense Department delegation to Taiwan to urge its acquisition of missile defense systems, including the PAC-3.[99] After Chen criticized the Patriot's performance in Operation Iraqi Freedom in 2003, a Pentagon spokesperson corrected Chen to Taiwan's media on March 27, 2003.[100] According to the U.S. Army, the Patriot missile defense system (with Guidance Enhanced Missiles (GEM) and PAC-3 missiles) intercepted nine Iraqi missiles out of nine engagements.[101] In April 2003, Taiwan submitted a request for price and availability data in a step towards a contract, and in May 2004, Defense Minister Lee Jye requested six PAC-3 firing units and upgrade of three PAC-2 Plus firing units (deployed around Taipei and not major military bases or assets) to the PAC-3 standard for about $4.3 billion.[102]

Complicated by the failure of a referendum to pass in March 2004, Taiwan's military looked to buy PAC-3 units, originally seeking funds out of a Special Budget submitted in May 2004.[103] Acquisition of missile defense systems was controversial in Taiwan, with some supporting the development of domestic long-range missiles instead and some preferring short-range missile defense systems. (See discussion below.) Missile defense also became politicized, when President Chen Shui-bian pushed for a referendum on buying more missile defense systems that was held on the presidential election day on March 20, 2004. That referendum became invalid when only 45% of eligible voters cast ballots (with 50% needed). (Out of the valid ballots cast, 92% agreed with the proposal.) The opposition KMT and PFP parties objected to acquiring PAC-3 missiles for three years, based on their claim that the referendum "vetoed" the question.[104]

---

[98] *Taiwan Defense Review*, December 6, 2002.

[99] *Central News Agency* (Taiwan), March 11, 2003.

[100] *Taipei Times*, March 29, 2003.

[101] U.S. Army, 32nd Army Air and Missile Defense Command, Fort Bliss, TX, "Operation Iraqi Freedom: Theater Air and Missile Defense," September 2003. For a skeptical view, see Randy Barrett, "Pentagon Releases Candid Glimpse of Missile Defense During Iraq War," *Space News*, November 10, 2003.

[102] *Far Eastern Economic Review*, May 15, 2003; *Jane's*, July 23, 2003; *Taiwan Defense Review*, June 15, 2004.

[103] *Central News Agency*, March 3, 2004; *China Times*, April 13, 2004; *Taiwan Defense Review*, April 30, 2004.

[104] A KMT lawmaker, Su Chi, voiced his objections to missile defense based on the referendum's result during the author's visit to Taiwan in October 2004, before his election.

In 2006, Taiwan's military and lawmakers debated whether to upgrade Taiwan's PAC-2 missile defense units, if PAC-3 missiles were not purchased. Legislative Yuan President Wang Jin-pyng promoted PAC-2 upgrades, but other KMT lawmakers did not support additional purchases of Patriot missile defense. KMT Legislator Shuai Hua-ming, a retired army lieutenant general, preferred more "cost-effective" weapons and "offensive" missile systems as "deterrence."[105] At the time, Taiwan had not upgraded its Patriot missile defense systems (to the latest configuration for radars and command and control with new training and hardware). The cheaper option to first upgrade the ground systems for Taiwan's three PAC-2 units was estimated at $600 million. In April 2006, after first rejecting Patriot upgrades, Taiwan's defense ministry requested U.S. price and availability data for PAC-2 upgrades and requested a supplemental budget for Patriot upgrades in 2006 (not passed).[106] In the end, Taiwan's LY deleted the defense ministry's request of about $347 million (out of a total program cost of $3.6 billion) to procure PAC-3 missiles in the 2007 defense budget passed on June 15, 2007, and opted to fund about $110 million for PAC-2 upgrades (out of a total program cost of $603 million). The President notified Congress in November 2007 of the proposed Patriot ground systems upgrade program, valued at $939 million.

In late 2007, Taiwan's LY partially resolved whether to procure PAC-3 missiles. In October 2007, the LY's defense committee retained a requested budget of about US$539 million in the 2008 defense budget to begin to procure PAC-3 missiles. However, the question was left for inter-party negotiations and the full LY to address in December 2007, which decided to fund four sets but freeze the funds for two more, freezing NT$5.8 billion (US$179 million) out of NT$17.5 billion (US$539 million). By the second quarter of 2008, the LY's Foreign Affairs and National Defense Committee released frozen funds, for the total program of six PAC-3 missile batteries with 384 missiles.[107] On October 3, 2008, President Bush notified Congress of a proposed sale of 330 PAC-3 missiles for $3.1 billion. However, the President broke up into two parts the sale of PAC-3 systems, excluding three of seven firing units (including one training unit) and about 50 missiles. The implications of this arbitrary decision included the requirement of a second notification of a second purchase as well as delays and a higher cost for Taiwan, with additional $2 billion. President Obama notified Congress on January 29, 2010, of a sale of the remaining three firing units with 114 PAC-3 missiles, for another program valued at $2.81 billion. Taiwan will have a total of ten Patriot batteries to fire PAC-2 GEM or PAC-3 missiles. Still, Taiwan needed early warning radars and a command, control, communications, and computers (C4) system.

## Early Warning Radar

In 1999, some in Congress encouraged the Clinton Administration to approve a sale of early warning radars, approval that was given in 2000. The Pentagon stressed the importance of long-range early warning and tracking of ballistic and cruise missile attacks against Taiwan. Taiwan reportedly considered two options: a radar similar to AN/FPS-115 Pave Paws sold by Raytheon and the LM Digital UHF Radar proposed by Lockheed Martin.[108] Despite divided opinions among lawmakers, in November 2003, Taiwan's legislature approved the Defense Ministry's request for about $800 million to fund one radar site (rather than an option for two).[109]

---

[105] *Taipei Times*, April 10, 2006; and author's interview with Shuai Hua-min in April 2006.

[106] *Central News Agency*, February 21, 2006; *Taipei Times*, February 22, 2006; author's interview with Raytheon in March 2006; and author's interviews in Taipei in April 2006.

[107] U.S.-Taiwan Business Council, "Defense & Security Report," Second Quarter 2008.

[108] *Jane's Defense Weekly*, March 26, 2003, and February 11, 2004.

[109] *Taiwan Defense Review*, November 26, 2003; *Jane's Defense Review*, December 3, 2003.

Nonetheless, on March 30, 2004, the Defense Department notified Congress of the proposed sale of two ultra high frequency long range early warning radars, with the potential value of $1.8 billion, that would enhance Taiwan's ability to identify and detect ballistic missiles as well as cruise missiles, and other threats from the air, and improve the early warning capability of Taiwan's C4ISR architecture. The notification pointed out that U.S. personnel would not be assigned to the radar(s). By early 2005, Taiwan had not contracted for the controversial program, and Lockheed Martin withdrew its bid.[110] In June 2005, Raytheon concluded a contract worth $752 million to provide one Early Warning Surveillance Radar System to Taiwan by September 2009.[111] However, by early 2007, Taiwan decided not to procure the second radar.[112] Construction of the radar in the Surveillance Radar Program (SRP) proceeded in 2009. It would set up a missile warning center with links to Taiwan's command authority and possibly the U.S. military.

However, Taiwan complained of mistrust, delays, and price increases for the SRP (and other programs). The U.S. Air Force unexpectedly asked Taiwan to agree to two revised Letters of Offer and Acceptance for two additional payments of about $141 million (requested in December 2007 to cover costs in disaster response) and about $56 million (requested in June 2009 to enhance anti-tampering). In 2011, Raytheon requested a third increase of about $200 million. While officials in Taiwan, including in the LY and Taiwan's military, expressed frustration at the extra U.S. demands, they said they remained committed to the SRP.[113]

## Command and Control

In addition, after approval in 1999, the United States has assisted Taiwan's command, control, communications, and computers (C4) program (named Po Sheng), intended to acquire datalinks and integration of the services into a joint system.[114] In July 2001, the Bush Administration notified Congress of a proposed sale of Joint Tactical Information Distribution Systems (JTIDS)/Link 16 terminals, a basis for an expanded program. In early 2003, the Administration signaled to Taiwan that this FMS program (managed by the U.S. Navy's SPAWAR command) should be given top priority. However, Taiwan opted for a program costing about $1.4 billion, rather than the comprehensive recommendation costing about $3.9 billion.[115] In September 2003, Lockheed Martin signed a contract with the initial value of $27.6 million.[116] The Administration's notification to Congress submitted on September 24, 2003, indicated that the total value could reach $775 million. Taiwan's Defense Ministry also decided not to integrate U.S. communications security (COMSEC) equipment that could facilitate crisis-management and interoperability.[117]

---

[110] *Jane's Defense Weekly*, February 9, 2005.

[111] Raytheon, June 23, 2005; Department of Defense, Air Force Contract for Raytheon, June 23, 2005; *Wall Street Journal*, June 24, 2005; *CNA*, June 25, 2005.

[112] Wendell Minnick, "Taiwan's Military Grapples with a Major C4ISR Upgrade," *C4ISR Journal*, March 2, 2007.

[113] Author's consultations with officials in Taipei in November 2009. Also see "Taiwan Pays NT$34 Billion on Behalf of the U.S. to Guard its Own Door," *I Chou Kan*, Taipei, October 22, 2009; Max Hirsch, "Taiwan 'Frustrated' with U.S. Over Key Radar and Other Arms Deals," *Kyodo*, November 4, 2009; *Liberty Times*, February 22, 2010; *Central News Agency*, June 14, 2011; *Taipei Times*, June 17, 2011.

[114] *Chung-Kuo Shih-Pao [China Times]* (Taiwan), July 18, 2001; *Defense and Aerospace* (U.S.-Taiwan Business Council), 2001; *Taiwan Defense Review*, August 27, 2002.

[115] SPAWAR briefing at U.S.-Taiwan Defense Industry Conference, February 12-14, 2003; *Taiwan Defense Review*, July 17, 2003; *Tzu-Yu Shih Pao* [Liberty Times], July 14, 2003.

[116] *Taiwan Defense Review*, September 17, 2003; *Jane's Defense Weekly*, October 1, 2003.

[117] U.S.-Taiwan Business Council, "Defense & Security Report," Third Quarter 2004.

---

Full Operational Capability of the initial Po Sheng program was reached at the end of 2009, after which Taiwan named the capability the Syun An C4 system.[118] (See below on the espionage case involving Taiwan's Army Major General Lo Hsien-che that compromised the Po Sheng system.)

In May 2009, Taiwan submitted a Letter of Request for follow-on technical support for this Po Sheng program (in 2010 to 2014). A program for Taiwan Integrated Support System (TISS) would not be a new system or capability. Taiwan would integrate more platforms, systems, and sensors in air, naval, and ground units to the Po Sheng command and control network.[119] President Obama notified Congress on January 29, 2010, of this follow-on support program.

Nonetheless, Taiwan acquired only one-third of the U.S.-recommended C4 network. A U.S. private sector study in 2010 stressed that Taiwan could invest more to leverage critical C4ISR for its "all-hazards defense" and warned that Taiwan's defense and homeland security officials lagged behind in leveraging the information technology (IT) that made Taiwan's companies major players in the global economy. Moreover, in early 2011, an ex-DSCA official urged Taiwan to work towards the complete integration of the C4 system with the Patriot missile defense units and the early warning radar (SRP). He critiqued Taiwan's efforts as "slowly" moving toward a credible missile defense capability that still required an expanded and integrated C4 network for early warning detection, tracking, and prioritization of missile threats.[120]

## AMRAAM and SLAMRAAM

In April 2000, the Clinton Administration approved the sale of AIM-120 Advanced Medium-Range Air-to-Air Missiles (AMRAAMs) to Taiwan, with the understanding that the missiles would be kept in storage on U.S. territory and transferred later to Taiwan, if/when the People's Liberation Army (PLA) acquires a similar Russian missile, like the R-77 (AA-12) air-to-air missile, or threatens to attack Taiwan. In September 2000, the Administration notified Congress of a potential sale of 200 AMRAAMs.

On July 1, 2002, the *Washington Times* reported that, in June, two SU-30 fighters of the PLA Air Force test-fired AA-12 medium-range air-to-air missiles acquired from Russia. The report raised questions as to whether the PLA already deployed the missiles. According to *Reuters* (July 10, 2002), Raytheon planned to finalize production of the AMRAAMs for Taiwan by the fall of 2003. Some in Congress urged the Administration to transfer AMRAAMs to Taiwan after production.

By the end of 2002, the Bush Administration authorized delivery of the AMRAAMs to Taiwan and briefed its Air Force on ground-launched AMRAAMs.[121] (The U.S. Army has developed the Surface Launched Advanced Medium Range Air-to-Air Missile, or SLAMRAAM, for cruise missile defense.) By November 2003, Taiwan received its first delivery of AMRAAMs, and a pilot of Taiwan's Air Force test-fired an AMRAAM at Tyndall Air Force Base in Florida on

---

[118] U.S.-Taiwan Business Council, defense industry conference, Charlottesville, VA, September 29, 2009.

[119] Author's consultation, September 2009.

[120] Mark Stokes, "Revolutionizing Taiwan's Security: Leveraging C4ISR for Traditional and Non-Traditional Challenges," Project 2049 Institute, February 19, 2010; Ed Ross (President of EWRoss International), "Taiwan's Ballistic-Missile Deterrence and Defense Capabilities," *China Brief*, Jamestown Foundation, February 10, 2011.

[121] *Lien-Ho Pao [United Daily News]*, Taipei, January 5, 2003; Remarks of Deputy Under Secretary of the Air Force Willard Mitchell at the U.S.-Taiwan Business Council's conference in February 2003.

---

November 10, 2003.[122] However, although the Clinton Administration agreed to Taiwan's request for 200 AMRAAMs for Taiwan's 150 F-16 fighters, Taiwan's Air Force actually purchased only 120 AMRAAMs (although some U.S. observers think Taiwan needs at least 350 AMRAAMs).[123] By April 2004, the Defense Department reportedly encouraged Taiwan to acquire the SLAMRAAM to help counter the PLA's expected deployment of land attack cruise missiles.[124]

## F-16C/D Fighters

Since 2006, Taiwan has been trying to request to procure new F-16C/D fighters, to add to its existing F-16 force. In 2006, Taiwan's Defense Ministry requested initial funding from the LY to acquire 66 F-16C/D fighters and to boost the defense budget in 2007 (an attempt to reach 2.85% of GDP).[125] On November 6, 2006, the LY's defense and budget committees jointly passed an amended 2007 defense budget, which froze the requested budget for F-16C/D fighters for five months (ending on May 31, 2007), pending U.S. provision of price and availability data. When the LY passed the final 2007 defense budget on June 15, 2007, the deadline for releasing the funds (about $488 million) for F-16C/Ds was extended until October 31. In the LY, there was broad political support for procurement of new fighters, but there was uncertainty about next steps if President Bush did not approve the release of pricing data (a potential sale).

The Bush Administration refused even to accept a formal Letter of Request (LOR) for F-16C/D fighters, after Taiwan tried to submit one in June-July 2006, February 2007, and June 2007.[126] Nonetheless, in October 2007, the LY's defense committee passed a 2008 defense budget that retained the requested F-16 procurement program. In December 2007, inter-party negotiations and the final decision in the LY deleted NT$2.2 billion from NT$22.2 billion leaving NT$20 billion (US$615 million). But the whole amount was frozen pending U.S. price and availability data. On September 22, 2008, Defense Minister Chen Chao-min reported to the LY that the military needed to acquire the new F-16 fighters. The Defense Ministry had to return the unspent funds in the 2007 defense budget and needed to return the funds in the 2008 budget.

In 2006, President Bush reportedly was reluctant to consider a formal request for new F-16 fighters without Taiwan's resolution of pending arms sales and without a 2007 defense budget that included funds for the fighters, given questions about Taiwan's credibility on arms purchases. Moreover, the Administration expressed disapproval in April 2007 about Taiwan's domestic development of land-attack cruise missiles (see discussion below). Then, within days after the LY's passage of the 2007 defense budget in mid-June 2007, Taiwan President Chen proposed a referendum on membership in the U.N. under the name "Taiwan" to be held on the day of the next presidential election (scheduled for March 22, 2008). At a U.S.-Taiwan defense industry conference on September 10-11, 2007, at which there was concern about the persisting status of

---

[122] *Taiwan Defense Review*, November 15, 2003; *Central News Agency*, November 18, 2003.

[123] Wendell Minnick, "Taiwan's Military will Fire Blanks," *Taipei Times*, May 25, 2005.

[124] *Jane's Defense Weekly*, April 7, 2004.

[125] In spring of 2006, Taiwan's Defense Ministry considered asking to purchase new F-16C/D (not F-15) fighters (author's interviews in Taipei in April 2006). Also: Wendell Minnick, "Airplane Race in Taiwan Straits," *Defense News*, May 15, 2006; Jim Wolf, "Taiwan Seeks 66 F-16 Fighters," *Reuters*, July 27, 2006; Minnick, "U.S. Debates Taiwan Request for 66 F-16s," *Defense News*, August 28, 2006; author's consultations in September 2006; and *Central News Agency*, Taipei, October 2, 2006 (quoting Minister Lee Jye).

[126] *Liberty Times*, Taipei, November 2, 2007; consultation with TECRO, February 29, 2008; and U.S.-Taiwan Business Council, "Defense & Security Report," Second Quarter 2008; *Central News Agency*, June 24, 2011.

"no decision" on whether to consider Taiwan's interest in new F-16s, the Administration issued a speech to stress U.S. opposition to this referendum while linking strength and moderation as two requirements for the broader and longer-term security of Taiwan.[127] President Bush looked to Beijing to cooperate in nuclear nonproliferation efforts targeting North Korea and Iran. After President George H. W. Bush approved the sale of 150 F-16A/B fighters to Taiwan in September 1992, the PRC ended its participation in the "Arms Control in the Middle East" talks and transferred M-11 short-range ballistic missiles to Pakistan in November 1992 (albeit either in retaliation or regardless of U.S. actions). Some critics argued that the sale in 1992 of F-16 fighters violated the 1982 Joint Communique on reducing arms sales to Taiwan and that continuing arms sales to Taiwan would harm U.S. ties with a rising China with greater wealth and influence. In addition to concerns about the impact on the U.S.-PRC relationship and cross-strait engagement, some questioned whether Taiwan's limited defense dollars might be better spent on other defense requirements, such as munitions, logistics, training, personnel, and other hardware for asymmetric advantages. Also, some raised concern about the limited impact of 66 new fighters on the military balance to counter the PLA's larger missile and other threats to Taiwan's aircraft and airfields.[128]

Advocates argued that Taiwan's legitimate requirement for F-16C/D fighters needed for air defense should not be linked to other programs or political considerations.[129] Taiwan was showing commitment to self-defense, a U.S. goal for cross-strait stability. Section 3(b) of the TRA stipulates that the President and Congress shall determine arms sales "based solely upon their judgment of the needs of Taiwan." In 1994, Congress passed the Foreign Relations Authorization Act for FY1994-FY1995 (P.L. 103-236), with language to affirm that Section 3 of the TRA (on arms sales) takes primacy over policy statements (1982 Joint Communique). Moreover, in issuing the August 17, 1982, Joint Communique, President Reagan wrote in a memo that "it is essential that the quantity and quality of the arms provided Taiwan be conditioned entirely on the threat posed by the PRC. Both in quantitative and qualitative terms, Taiwan's defense capability relative to that of the PRC will be maintained." Further, supporters argued that the United States should consider Taiwan's request when Taiwan showed a commitment to raise its defense capabilities and the KMT Party's Ma Ying-jeou became president in May 2008 with the goal to resume cross-strait talks to reduce tension. Also, withholding support for this request would undermine another U.S. objective of discouraging Taiwan's deployment of cruise missiles. In addition, supporters pointed out that in April 2001, President Bush dropped the 20-year-old annual arms talks used to discuss arms sales in favor of depoliticized determinations of Taiwan's requests on an as-needed basis. Taiwan cited a need to replace obsolete fighters. Selling more F-16s to Taiwan would affect Taiwan's air defense beyond the number of 66 planes and upgrade overall capabilities that include pilots (whom the U.S. Air Force has trained), when Taiwan's defense capabilities matter for deterrence in peacetime as well as in a conflict. Just after retiring as the Air Force's Deputy Under Secretary for International Affairs, Bruce Lemkin said in July 2010 that new F-16 fighters would help Taiwan to maintain the same deterrent capability that the United States helped Taiwan to

---

[127] Deputy Assistant Secretary of State Thomas Christensen, "A Strong and Moderate Taiwan," U.S.-Taiwan Defense Industry Conference, Annapolis, MD, September 11, 2007.

[128] Chas. Freeman, Jr., "Preventing War in the Taiwan Strait," *Foreign Affairs*, July/August 1998; Rand Corporation, "Turning the Tide: Analysis of Military Modernization Options for Taiwan," a study for the U.S. Defense Department and Taiwan's Defense Ministry, September 2009; Bill Owens (retired admiral and co-chair of unofficial "Sanya Talks" with the PLA), "America Must Start Treating China as a Friend," *Financial Times*, November 17, 2009.

[129] U.S.-Taiwan Business Council, "Defense & Security Report," 3rd Quarter 2006, 2nd Quarter 2007, and "The Balance of Air Power in the Taiwan Strait," May 2010; John Tkacik, "Approve Taiwan Arms Buy," *Defense News*, July 30, 2007; Dean Cheng, "Meeting Taiwan's Self-Defense Needs," Heritage Foundation, February 26, 2010.

achieve in the late 1990s.[130] On October 4, 2011, six retired Air Force lieutenant generals and generals and a former Secretary of the Air Force wrote to Senators John Cornyn and Robert Menendez to support a sale of F-16C/Ds to help restore the military balance, increase stability, and decrease the likelihood of any U.S. intervention between the PRC and Taiwan.[131]

Days after Taiwan's presidential election in March 2008, Under Secretary of Defense for Policy Eric Edelman promised Senators Tim Johnson and James Inhofe of the Senate Taiwan Caucus that the department would consider carefully any request from Taiwan for defense articles and services, "including replacement airframes."[132] Nevertheless, some were concerned that the Bush Administration stressed China's objections over U.S. policy consideration of arms sales based solely upon Taiwan's legitimate defense needs. Even after Taiwan approved a defense budget in December 2007 and Ma Ying-jeou succeeded Chen Shui-bian as Taiwan's president in May 2008, President Bush continued to rebuff Taiwan's efforts to request F-16 fighters, in part because of the Olympic Games in August 2008.[133]

U.S. policy has long helped Taiwan to maintain its Air Force capabilities. In January 1982, President Ronald Reagan decided to sell F-5E fighters, as they were more advanced than the PRC's fighters at the time, and to consider the more sophisticated F-5G version if Taiwan needed them.[134] The F-16C/D (single-seat/two-seat versions) multi-role (air-to-air and air-to-surface combat) fighters would not be a new type of weapon sold to Taiwan, as they are the improved versions of F-16s sold in 1992. In September 1992, President George H. W. Bush notified Congress of the sale of 150 F-16A/B fighters with a value of $5.8 billion. (The first F-16A fighters entered service in the U.S. Air Force in 1979. In 1980, the Air Force began a program to improve the F-16's capabilities for precision strike, night attack, and beyond-visual-range interception, with advanced controls and fire control radars. The U.S. Air Force received the first F-16C fighters in 1984.)[135] As discussed above, the U.S. Air Force has invested efforts in a program to train Taiwan's F-16 pilots at Luke Air Force Base, AZ, since 1997, and had concerns when Taiwan's defense minister considered ending the training program in 2004.

Since 1990, the PLA Air Force has bought Russian Su-27 and Su-30 fighters, and in late 2006, received the first J-10 fighters (developed in China based on the Israeli Lavi program of the 1980s). The PLA Air Force also acquired Russian S-300PMU2 surface-to-air missiles with a range that extends over Taiwan's airspace. The Secretary of Defense's annual report to Congress on PRC military power warned in 2009 that the modernizing PLA continued to shift the cross-strait military balance in its favor and that it was no longer the case that Taiwan's Air Force enjoyed dominance of the airspace over the strait. The Pentagon reported to Congress in 2011 that the PLA Air Force deployed 490 combat aircraft (330 fighters and 160 bombers) within range of Taiwan (without need to refuel), while Taiwan had 388 fighters and 22 bombers. However, these numbers do not depict the dynamic situation, in which deployments and readiness could change. Taiwan's Air Force has deployed 145 F-16A/B fighters (with 14 of them at Luke Air Force Base

---

[130] Quoted by Jim Wolf, "Taiwan Overdue for F-16 Jets, Ex-U.S. Official Said," *Reuters*, July 6, 2010.

[131] Signed by David Deptula, Michael Dunn, John Loh, William Looney, Lester Lyles, Lloyd Newton, and Michael Wynne.

[132] Eric Edelman, letter in response to Senators Tim Johnson and James Inhofe, March 28, 2008.

[133] *Washington Times*, May 9 and 30, 2008; Rupert Hammond-Chambers, President of the U.S.-Taiwan Business Council, "Taiwan's Security on Hold," op-ed, *The Hill*, June 6, 2008.

[134] Ronald Reagan, *The Reagan Diaries* (Harper Collins Publishers, 2007).

[135] *Jane's All the World's Aircraft, 1986-1987*; U.S. Air Force fact sheet, June 2006.

for training), 127 Indigenous Defense Fighters (IDFs) (with limited combat range and payload capacity), 56 Mirage-2000 fighters (with costly spares and support that led to reduced readiness and consideration of mothballing them by 2009), and 32 F-5s (that still fly for training though they reached the end of their operational life). Taiwan asserted a need to replace aging F-5s but actually also needs to replace the IDFs and Mirage fighters (bought from France in 1992).[136]

Taiwan included $82 million for the F-16C/D program in the 2009 defense budget, for a total cost estimated at $4.7 billion. In public remarks on April 22, 2009, President Ma Ying-jeou reiterated his commitment to the Obama Administration that Taiwan still requested the F-16C/Ds. By mid-2009, Taiwan quietly admitted difficulty in sustaining costly maintenance of the Mirage fighters, but Taiwan's Air Force denied in October 2010 earlier reports that it had to mothball the Mirages. Without a U.S. decision through 2009 on whether to consider Taiwan's request for F-16C/Ds (despite Taiwan's funding in defense budgets), 26 of Taiwan's legislators, led by Shuai Hua-ming, sent a letter to the Congress in early January 2010 to express their bipartisan commitment to the request. On January 29, 2010, when President Obama submitted his first notifications to Congress on arms sales to Taiwan, Administration officials noted that they were still assessing Taiwan's requirement for fighters.

In 2010, Lockheed Martin stressed the urgency of a new sale of F-16 fighters to Taiwan, because it would help keep the production line open as the F-16 program was drawing to an end. The manufacturing process would need contracts three years before the production line closes, in part to sustain sub-contracts for supplies. By 2020, Taiwan's fighters would drop in number by 70% without new F-16s and by 50% with 66 new F-16s. Lockheed Martin also commissioned a study released in June 2011 that estimated a program of F-16s for Taiwan with direct spending of about $4.6 billion with 23,407 direct jobs in 44 states and the District of Columbia (while generating about $8.7 billion in total output and 87,664 in total jobs when including indirect employment).[137] Still, Taiwan was not the only interested buyer of F-16s. Aside from commercial considerations, a concern for policymakers would be the dim chance of an alternative if the F-16 is no longer available. Moreover, years after Taiwan first asked for F-16C/Ds, the issue evolved to the U.S. response to deterioration in Taiwan's whole air force, beyond whether to sell more planes. In an address to the United States on May 12, 2011, President Ma reiterated Taiwan's need to buy F-16C/D fighters and submarines, primarily for leverage in political negotiations with Beijing. Ma was running for reelection in January 2012, and his campaign manager, King Pu-tsung, visited Washington where on September 11, he called U.S. arms "bargaining chips" with the PRC. Meanwhile, visiting Deputy Minister of Defense Andrew Yang said in Richmond on September 18 that Taiwan also looks to procure the more advanced F-35 fighters. He called the F-16C/Ds and submarines the most urgent systems for Taiwan to acquire (not the F-16A/B upgrade).

On September 21, 2011, the Administration did not provide answers about whether to sell new F-16C/Ds (though it said that it did not rule out a sale) or why it still would not accept Taiwan's formal request, while notifying Congress of a program to upgrade Taiwan's existing F-16A/B fighters. Though President Ma politically and publicly thanked President Obama for the upgrade of F-16A/Bs, Ma told visiting Representative Hank Johnson on September 30 that the F-16A/B

---

[136] Secretary of Defense, "Military Power of the People's Republic of China, 2009," March 25, 2009; "Taiwan Air Defense Status Assessment," DIA-02-1001-028, dated January 21, 2010; and "Military and Security Developments Involving the People's Republic of China, 2011," August 24, 2011; Author's consultations.

[137] Lockheed Martin's briefing, March 23, 2010; Perryman Group, "An Assessment of the Potential Impact of the Lockheed Martin Taiwan F-16 Program on Business Activity in Affected States and Congressional Districts," 2011.

program was needed because of obsolete spare parts but Taiwan still needs new F-16C/Ds to replace aging fighters. (Also see Johnson's commentary in *The Hill* on October 11, 2011.)

## F-16A/B Upgrade

Another consideration arose after Taiwan submitted a Letter of Request in November 2009 to upgrade its F-16A/B fighters sold back in 1992. Taiwan argued this program would be necessary in parallel to and not a substitute for new F-16C/D fighters. The program for existing F-16A/B fighters would upgrade them, extend their service life, and meet problems of obsolete spare parts, but would not add new planes to replace old fighters. The Ma Administration's and LY's priorities were for new F-16C/Ds, not for only an upgrade. One issue has concerned whether and how Taiwan would fund both programs. Taiwan could request additional upgraded F-16A/B fighters.

In August 2011, the United States provided pricing data, and Taiwan's military requested allocations from the LY beginning in the 2012 defense budget for a total of $3.8 billion.[138] On September 21, the Administration formally notified Congress of three programs to upgrade Taiwan's 145 F-16A/Bs (for $5.3 billion), continue to train Taiwan's F-16 pilots at Luke Air Force Base, and to sell spare parts for F-16A/Bs, F-5E/Fs, C-130Hs, and IDFs. The program to upgrade, or retrofit, the F-16A/Bs was more extensive and expensive than earlier expectations, including new active electronically scanned array (AESA) radars and JDAMs. Options include Northrop Grumman's AN/APG-80 AESA radar and Raytheon's AESA Advanced Combat Radar. At a U.S.-Taiwan defense industry conference on September 19, Acting Assistant Secretary of Defense Peter Lavoy stressed Taiwan's need for survivable, credible deterrence. Separately, in two briefings issued by the State Department on September 19 and 21, even before and on the day of the formal notification to and public announcement of confidential consultations with Congress, the Obama Administration shaped reporting by the press. The Administration asserted that the President's decision to upgrade the F-16A/Bs will provide "essentially the same quality as new F-16C/D aircraft at a far cheaper price" and that Taiwan would get 145 F-16A/Bs instead of only 66 F-16C/Ds. The Administration said that the upgrade would make an "immediate and significant contribution" to Taiwan's air defense and that the F-16A/B program would "get greater capabilities more rapidly in a larger number of airplanes into the field in a more decisive way in this context, again, without ruling out any future sales."

However, the Administration's assertions raised many questions. Taiwan would not get any additional planes to replace fighters. The cost was higher than previous estimates of about $2 billion-$4.5 billion, or perhaps 55%-65% of new F-16s.[139] The Administration did not explain why it decided on a program for F-16A/Bs but not a program for new F-16C/Ds, if they are all vulnerable to the PLA's missile attacks. Moreover, according to Lockheed Martin, the retrofit would take one squadron (about 24) of Taiwan's F-16A/B fighters out of service at a time over five years. The retrofit would not start until 2017, after five years of preparatory work. The program would take three years longer than a program to sell the same number of 145 new F-16C/D fighters, which would take seven years. The program did not include new engines, which if included would have increased the cost and given the F-16s better performance. Taiwan's Ministry of National Defense responded that the F-16A/B retrofit and the F-16C/D procurement would meet different requirements, that the retrofit program would bring the F-16A/B's

---

[138] *Defense News*, August 14, 2011; *Central News Agency*, September 1, 2011; *Taipei Times*, September 2, 2011.

[139] Consultations; and Wendell Minnick, "Taiwan Frustrated Over Stalled F-16 Effort," *Defense News*, April 1, 2011.

---

capabilities to 80% of those of F-16C/Ds, that some capabilities will be upgraded to be better than those of the U.S. Air Force's F-16 C/Ds, and that the cost would be budgeted over 12 years. Moreover, more of Taiwan's Air Force would be out of service, as it has upgraded in Taiwan 71 of the 127 IDFs (for completion in 2012) and plans to upgrade the other 56 IDFs (in 2013-2017).

## Other Possible Future Sales

In addition to the major weapon systems discussed above, possible future arms sales to Taiwan's military include:[140]

- signals intelligence (SIGINT) aircraft (perhaps from Gulfstream, Raytheon, or Cessna) for which Taiwan requested price and availability data in 2002;

- C-27J Spartan medium transport aircraft (sold by L3 Communications);

- F-35 Joint Strike Fighters (JSF), particularly the short take-off/vertical landing (STOVL) version, produced by Lockheed Martin and foreign partners;

- Stryker armored wheeled vehicles (sold by General Dynamics);

- upgraded engines for F-16s (Pratt & Whitney or General Electric);

- CH-53X minesweeping helicopters (developed by Sikorsky);

- T-6C trainer aircraft to replace T-34C trainers (sold by Hawker Beechcraft);

- KC-135 Stratotanker aerial refueling aircraft;

- Phalanx Close-In Weapons System (CIWS) (sold by Raytheon);

- Sensor Fuse Weapon for the Air Force (sold by Textron Systems);

- Armor Security Vehicle for the Military Police (sold by Textron Systems);

- HH-60G Pave Hawk helicopters;

- Upgrades of Lafayette-class frigates, other ships, and Sea Dragon submarines;

- Air traffic control system for Taiwan's Air Force (sold by ITT);

- Perry-class frigates (as Excess Defense Articles from the U.S. Navy);

- Newport-class landing ship tank (as Excess Defense Articles);

- Athena C4ISR situational awareness system (offered by Raytheon);

- Aegis Ashore, land-based missile defense system (by Lockheed Martin); and

- Sky Warrior tactical unmanned aerial vehicle (UAV) (sold by General Atomics).

---

[140] Author's consultations; and *Flight International*, November 25-December 1, 2003; *Jane's Defense Review*, January 14, 2004; U.S.-Taiwan Business Council, *Defense and Aerospace Report*, First Quarter 2004; *Taiwan Defense Review*, May 7, 2004; *CNA*, June 21, 2004; *Flight International*, July 13-19, 2004; *Flight International*, September 7-13, 2004; *Flight International*, December 7-13, 2004; *Taiwan Defense Review*, December 30, 2004; *AFP*, Hong Kong, March 8, 2005; *Jane's Defense Weekly*, May 4, 2005; *Defense News*, May 7, 2007; *Taipei Times*, June 24, 2007; *Lien-ho Pao*, July 9, 2007; *Defense News*, April 27, 2009; *JDW*, May 21, 2009; *Defense News*, June 15, August 17, 2009; *Aviation Week & Space Technology*, September 14, 2009; *CNA*, January 11, 2010; and *Defense News*, February 1, 2010.

# Policy Issues for Congress

Since the early 1990s, and accelerated after the Taiwan Strait crisis of 1995-1996, the PLA has modernized with a missile buildup and foreign arms acquisitions, primarily from Russia.[141] As a result of the PLA's provocative exercises and missile test-firings in 1995 and 1996 that were directed against Taiwan, Congress has increasingly asserted its role vis-a-vis the Administration in determining security assistance for Taiwan, as stipulated by Section 3(b) of the TRA, as well as in exercising its oversight of Section 2(b)(6) of the TRA on the U.S. capacity to resist any resort to force or other forms of coercion against Taiwan. Congress increasingly asserted its role in determining arms sales to Taiwan *before* sales were decided. An added issue, particularly since 2008, has concerned the process for considering Taiwan's requests and notifications to Congress.

Moreover, Section 3(c) of the TRA requires the President to inform Congress "promptly" of any threat to "the security or the social or economic system" of the people on Taiwan and any danger to U.S. interests, so that the President together with the Congress shall determine the appropriate U.S. response. Nonetheless, in March 1996, during the Taiwan Strait Crisis when President Clinton deployed two aircraft carrier battle groups near Taiwan, the State Department testified that the situation did not constitute a "threat to the security or the social or economic system" of Taiwan and did not invoke Section 3(c) for a congressional role.[142] Policy issues center on how effectively the Administration has helped Taiwan's self-defense, the role of Congress in determining security assistance to Taiwan, and whether aspects of U.S. security assistance are stabilizing or destabilizing and should be adjusted based on changing conditions. Overall, the question for policy has concerned whether to disengage from or increase engagement with Taiwan in a number of specific areas.

## Extent of U.S. Commitment to Help Taiwan's Self-Defense

The persistent question for U.S. decision-makers in the military, Administration, and Congress is whether the United States would go to war with the PRC over Taiwan and the purpose of any conflict. The question of U.S. assistance for Taiwan's defense involves two aspects: intention (political commitment) and military capability to assist Taiwan's self-defense. The TRA did not replace the Mutual Defense Treaty of 1954 that ended in 1979. Nonetheless, some have called for a clear commitment (to shore up deterrence and help Taiwan's self-defense), advanced arms sales, interoperability with Taiwan's military, combined operational training and planning, high-level meetings, and visits by U.S. flag and general officers to Taiwan. Others have argued that the United States should avoid a war with China and needs a cooperative China to address a number of global problems and that the United States should reconsider arms sales to Taiwan (either as leverage against political moves or as a hindrance to a political settlement). Another option would be to limit U.S. assistance to arms sales and related transfers while not committing U.S. forces.

In March 1996, President Clinton deployed two aircraft carrier battle groups near Taiwan in response to the PLA's provocative missile test-firings and exercises in the Taiwan Strait Crisis of 1995-1996. Another question arose in April 2001 when President Bush initially said that he would do "whatever it took to help Taiwan defend herself" if China attacked.

---

[141] See the Defense Department's annual reports to Congress on PRC Military Power.

[142] Assistant Secretary of State for East Asian and Pacific Affairs Winston Lord, before the House International Relations Subcommittee on Asia and the Pacific, hearing on "Crisis in the Taiwan Strait: Implications for U.S. Foreign Policy," March 14, 1996, 104th Congress.

Supporters viewed such clarity as needed to prevent miscalculations in Beijing and deter attacks against Taiwan. However, critics argued that Bush encouraged provocations from Taipei, even if the message was not meant for Taiwan, and weakened willingness in Taiwan to strengthen its own defense. Later, when Taiwan's President Chen Shui-bian advocated referendums and a new constitution, President Bush said that "the comments and actions made by the leader of Taiwan indicate that he may be willing to make decisions unilaterally to change the status quo, which we oppose," in appearing with PRC Premier Wen Jiabao in the Oval Office on December 9, 2003.

At a hearing in April 2004, in answer to Representative Gary Ackerman's questions about whether President Bush's phrase on "whatever it took to help Taiwan defend herself" meant that the United States would go to war with China if Taiwan made unilateral moves toward independence, Assistant Secretary James Kelly stated that what the president said had a meaning "at the time he says it to those listeners," the United States intended to fulfill the responsibilities under the TRA "to the extent necessary," the United States opposed "actions that would unilaterally alter Taiwan's status," leaders in Taiwan "misunderstood" if they believed that President Bush supported whatever they did, and "decisions of war and peace are made by the president with consultation with Congress." Assistant Secretary of Defense Peter Rodman replied that President Bush's phrase was a reaffirmation of the TRA, which left a certain "ambiguity." Rodman also warned Beijing that its use of force would "inevitably" involve the United States.[143]

In December 2004, Deputy Secretary of State Richard Armitage also clarified the U.S. defense commitment by saying, "we have the requirement with the Taiwan Relations Act to keep sufficient force in the Pacific to be able to deter attack. We are not required to defend. And these are questions that actually reside with the U.S. Congress, who has to declare an act of war."[144]

On June 8, 2005, President Bush qualified U.S. assistance for Taiwan's self-defense by saying that "If China were to invade unilaterally, we would rise up in the spirit of the Taiwan Relations Act. If Taiwan were to declare independence unilaterally, it would be a unilateral decision, that would then change the U.S. equation, the U.S. look at ... the decision-making process."[145]

In September 2005, the Defense Department further clarified the mutual obligations under the TRA and limits to the U.S. ability to assist Taiwan. Deputy Under Secretary of Defense Richard Lawless issued a speech, stressing the TRA's focus on Taiwan's self-defense. He declared that,

> inherent in the intent and logic of the TRA is the expectation that Taiwan will be able to mount a viable self-defense. For too long, the Taiwan Relations Act has been referenced as purely a U.S. obligation.... Under the TRA, the U.S. is obligated to "enable" Taiwan to maintain a sufficient self-defense, but the reality is, it is Taiwan that is obligated to have a sufficient self-defense. There is an explicit expectation in the TRA that Taiwan is ready, willing, and able to maintain its self-defense. Taiwan must fulfill its unwritten, but clearly evident obligations under the Taiwan Relations Act by appropriately providing for its own defense while not simply relying on the U.S.'s capacity to address a threat in the Strait. The TRA requires both parties to do their part to deter aggression or coercion vis-a-vis Taiwan.[146]

---

[143] House International Relations Committee, "The Taiwan Relations Act: The Next 25 Years," April 21, 2004.

[144] Richard Armitage, Interview with PBS, December 10, 2004.

[145] President George W. Bush, "Your World with Neil Cavuto," *Fox News*, June 8, 2005.

[146] A DSCA official, Ed Ross, read the speech on September 19, 2005, in San Diego, CA, at the Defense Industry Conference of the U.S.-Taiwan Business Council, while Lawless was delayed in Beijing at the Six-Party Talks on North Korea's nuclear weapons.

---

A co-chair of the House Taiwan Caucus, Representative Steve Chabot, stated on September 27, 2005, at the Heritage Foundation that Taiwan was only one ally and that it was principally Taiwan's responsibility to defend itself. He said that it was "frustrating" and "disappointing" to many Members of Congress that Taiwan delayed passage of the Special Budget on arms procurement. He warned that if Taiwan did not pass the Special Budget, many Members of Congress would "re-evaluate the extent of support for Taiwan."

Taiwan's President Chen Shui-bian announced on February 27, 2006, that he would "terminate" the National Unification Council, again raising questions about new tensions. Senator John Warner, chairman of the Armed Services Committee, told Admiral William Fallon, PACOM Commander, at a hearing on March 7, 2006, that "if conflict were precipitated by just inappropriate and wrongful politics generated by the Taiwanese elected officials, I'm not entirely sure that this nation would come full force to their rescue if they created that problem." On April 24, 2007, at a hearing of the Senate Armed Services Committee with the new PACOM commander, Admiral Timothy Keating, Senator Warner said Taiwan should not play the "TRA card" when the U.S. military was engaged heavily in the world.

After the KMT's Ma Ying-jeou became President in May 2008, he resumed cross-strait dialogue for the first time in a decade and pursued closer economic and other engagement with the PRC. Aside from contrasting with the cross-strait tension under his predecessor who was perceived as pushing for Taiwan's de jure independence, President Ma went further in May 2010 when he ruled out possible U.S. military deployments to help Taiwan's self-defense. Ma said that Taiwan will continue to purchase U.S. weapons, while Taiwan "will never ask the Americans to fight for Taiwan." In addition to stating this point in a reporter's interview, President Ma reiterated this stance in an attempt to assure visiting Senator Dianne Feinstein the next month.[147]

## Changes in PLA Missile Deployments and Other CBMs

There has been interest among U.S. academic circles and think tanks for Washington to pursue talks with Beijing on its military buildup and U.S. arms sales to Taiwan (instead of simply enhancing security assistance to Taiwan).[148] One catalyst for this debate arose out of the U.S.-PRC summit in Crawford, TX, on October 25, 2002. As confirmed to Taiwan's legislature by its envoy to Washington, C.J. Chen, and reported in Taiwan's media, then-PRC ruler Jiang Zemin offered in vague terms a freeze or reduction in China's deployment of missiles targeted at Taiwan, in return for restraint in U.S. arms sales to Taiwan.[149] President Bush reportedly did not respond directly to Jiang's linkage. Editorials in Taiwan were divided on whether to pursue Jiang's offer.

Some argued that confidence building measures (CBMs), such as a reduction in actual deployments of the PLA's missile and other units, would improve the chances for cross-strait political dialogue on Taiwan's status and lead to sustained stability. They said that the United

---

[147] President Ma's interview with *CNN*, published on May 1, 2010; author's consultation, Taipei, June 2010.

[148] See David Lampton and Richard Daniel Ewing, "U.S.-China Relations in a Post-September 11th World," Nixon Center, August 2002; David Shambaugh's arguments at conference by Carnegie Endowment, Stanford University, Center for Strategic and International Studies, and National Committee on U.S.-China Relations, on "Taiwan and U.S. Policy: Toward Stability or Crisis?," October 9, 2002; Michael Swaine, "Reverse Course? The Fragile Turnaround in U.S.-China Relations," Carnegie Endowment Policy Brief, February 2003; David Lampton, "The Stealth Normalization of U.S.-China Relations," *National Interest*, Fall 2003; Michael Swaine, "China, Taiwan, U.S.: Status Quo Challenged," *National Interest*, October 11, 2011.

[149] *Chung-Kuo Shih-Pao [China Times]*, Taipei, November 22, 2002; *Taipei Times*, November 23, 2002.

States could explore or even negotiate with the PRC how it might reduce the threat against Taiwan, such as dismantling missile brigades in a verifiable manner, since sales of U.S. systems are based on Taiwan's defense needs. They argued that Jiang's offer represented the first time that the PRC offered meaningfully to discuss its forces opposite Taiwan. Others said that a freeze or redeployment of missiles would not eliminate the PRC's continuing and broader military threat against Taiwan (including mobile missiles that can be re-deployed) and that the PRC should hold direct talks with leaders in Taipei instead. They argued that Jiang did not seek to reduce the PLA's coercive threat but to undermine the relationship between Washington and Taipei, including arms sales which take years to complete. They noted that the PLA's missile buildup has continued.

One issue for congressional oversight has concerned whether and how the President might deal with Beijing on the question of U.S. arms sales to Taiwan in the context of increasing cross-strait dialogue. Policy considerations include the TRA, the 1982 Joint Communique (which discussed reductions in U.S. arms sales to Taiwan premised on the PRC's peaceful unification policy), and the 1982 "Six Assurances" to Taiwan (including one of not holding prior consultations with the PRC on U.S. arms sales to Taiwan). At a hearing in March 2001, Secretary of State Colin Powell assured Senator Helms that the "Six Assurances" would remain U.S. policy and that the Administration would not favor consulting the PRC on arms sales to Taiwan.[150] The Bush Administration reportedly did not counter Jiang's verbal offer, noting the accelerated missile buildup, continued military threats against Taiwan, the need for the PRC to talk directly to Taiwan, the TRA, and the "Six Assurances" to Taiwan. Nonetheless, in April 2004, Assistant Secretary of State James Kelly testified at a hearing that if the PRC meets its stated obligations to pursue a peaceful resolution of the Taiwan issue and matches its rhetoric with a military posture that bolsters and supports peaceful approaches to Taiwan, "it follows logically that Taiwan's defense requirements will change."[151] In May 2005, an official PRC newspaper reported that the PLA continued to debate the question of whether to "withdraw" missiles opposite Taiwan.[152]

China has continued its buildup of short-range ballistic missiles, whose "adequate precision guidance" could destroy key leadership facilities, military bases, and communication and transportation nodes with "minimal advanced warning," warned the Pentagon's 2004 annual report to Congress on PRC military power. Later, the Secretary of Defense reported to Congress that by late 2008, the PLA deployed opposite Taiwan an arsenal of 1,050-1,150 mobile M-9 and M-11 short-range ballistic missiles (SRBMs).[153] That build-up increased by 60-80 SRBMs from 2007, less than the previously reported increase of about 100 missiles a year. At a hearing of the Senate Appropriations Subcommittee on Defense on June 16, 2010, Senator Feinstein asked Defense Secretary Robert Gates about any changes in China's military posture against Taiwan, and he testified that there continued to be an "extraordinary" deployment by the PLA of cruise as well as ballistic missiles opposite Taiwan, despite closer cross-strait engagement since 2008. The Secretary's report submitted in August 2011 estimated that the PLA deployed 1,000-1,200 SRBMs opposite Taiwan by the end of 2010. While the number of SRBMs remained constant, the more advanced missiles have precision strike capability with longer ranges, better accuracy, and various conventional warheads. Moreover a private study found in 2010 that the PRC has the

---

[150] Senate Foreign Relations Committee, Hearing on U.S. Foreign Policy, March 8, 2001.

[151] House International Relations Committee, "The Taiwan Relations Act: The Next 25 Years," April 21, 2004.

[152] *Qingnian Cankao [Youth Reference News]*, Beijing, May 26, 2005.

[153] Secretary of Defense, "Annual Report on the Military Power of the People's Republic of China," May 29, 2004, and "Military Power of the People's Republic of China, 2009," March 25, 2009.

world's largest force of ground-launched land attack cruise missiles (LACMs), with about 100 LACMs entering the operational force each year.[154]

Potential CBMs between the PLA and Taiwan's Ministry of National Defense (MND) gained momentum after the KMT's Ma Ying-jeou became President in Taipei in May 2008 and Hu Jintao in Beijing issued a speech in December 2008 with six points that included a proposal similar to Ma's, namely, "to end the state of hostility and reach a peace agreement, including exploring the establishment of a mechanism of mutual trust for military security." (Top ruler Hu Jintao is the Communist Party of China (CPC)'s General-Secretary, the Chairman of the Central Military Commission (CMC), and the President of the PRC.) There are many possible steps that could constitute CBMs, including changes in the PLA's deployment of some ballistic missiles.

One issue for U.S. policy concerns how the increasing cross-strait dialogue concerning and potential conduct of such CBMs positively and negatively might affect U.S. interests, with or without Taipei's consultation with Washington. Another issue asks whether the United States should encourage or play another role in the increasing cross-strait dialogues that potentially include such CBMs. In September 2009, Deputy Secretary of State James Steinberg stated that the Obama Administration "encouraged" the PRC and Taiwan to explore CBMs that would lead to closer ties and greater stability across the strait. His encouragement of CBMs raised expectations of an active U.S. role and injected new U.S. pressure in a sensitive domestic debate in Taiwan over whether such CBMs are premature at this time and would serve Taiwan's security interests. In contrast, later in the month, Assistant Secretary of Defense for Asian and Pacific Security Affairs Wallace Gregson said that "we are encouraged by the PRC's reciprocity in encouraging renewed interactions in cultural and economic affairs, but we have not yet seen similar progress or dialogue in military affairs. We encourage both sides to consider such steps at the appropriate time and in a mutually agreed manner." Gregson also urged Taiwan to stress "asymmetrical advantages" in its defense. Deputy Assistant Secretary of State for East Asian and Pacific Affairs David Shear echoed those measured words, saying that his department did not want to push Taiwan to hold CBMs and that they should occur at a pace acceptable to Taiwan's people. At a summit in Beijing in November, Presidents Obama and Hu issued a Joint Statement in which the United States did not use "encouragement" of cross-strait CBMs. As worded, the United States "welcomes the peaceful development of relations across the Taiwan Strait and looks forward to efforts by both sides to increase dialogues and interactions in economic, political, and other fields, and develop more positive and stable cross-Strait relations."[155]

Presidents Ma and Hu's proposals for CBMs and a "peace accord" have been considered in a controversial debate in Taiwan (including between civilian and military officials) concerning whether CBMs with the PLA serve Taiwan's security interests and whether those interests are better served in securing U.S. arms and other defense-related support that Taiwan's officials believe are necessary for the confidence to deal with Beijing. Some in Taiwan worry that CBMs with the PLA could lead to the PLA's stronger leverage at the expense of U.S.-Taiwan defense-related ties. There is also the question of whether Taiwan's expectations of a greater U.S. role could be met. In October 2009, Shuai Hua-ming, a key KMT Member of the Legislative Yuan in Taipei who is a retired Lieutenant General of the Army, questioned the U.S. commitment to help

---

[154] Project 2049, "Evolving Aerospace Trends in the Asia-Pacific Region," May 25, 2010.

[155] James Steinberg, "Administration's Vision of the U.S.-China Relationship," September 24, 2009; Wallace Gregson, "Remarks to the U.S.-Taiwan Business Council Defense Industry Conference," September 28, 2009; White House, "U.S.-China Joint Statement," November 17, 2009.

Taiwan's self-defense under the TRA (with delays and cost increases in arms programs), the push by some in Taiwan to build trust through triangular talks among Taiwan, China, and the United States (rather than traditional trust between Taiwan and the United States), and the will of Taiwan's military leadership to reform with new concepts of training, jointness, warfighting, and strategy (not simply using defensive weapons with no combat experience for decades).[156]

On November 2, 2009, the international Sun Tzu conference took place in Beijing with the attendance of Jia Qinglin, a Member of the Standing Committee of the Politburo of the CPC and with discussion of cross-strait CBMs. The PLA's Major General Luo Yuan of the Academy of Military Science (AMS) and a few of Taiwan's retired generals attended the conference.[157] On November 13-14, organizations with ties to officials of the two sides of the strait held the first conference in Taiwan to discuss economic, political, and security engagement, including CBMs and a peace accord. The PRC delegation attending the conference called "60 Years Across the Taiwan Strait" included Zheng Bijian, former vice president of the CPC's Central Party School, Yu Keli of the Institute of Taiwan Studies, retired Major General Pan Zhenqiang of the PLA's National Defense University, and retired PLA Lieutenant General Li Jijun of the Association for the Study of Sun Tzu's Art of War (and formerly at AMS and the CMC's General Office). Li Jijun said that the two sides could discuss the PLA's missiles only based on the "1992 Consensus" (rephrasing of "one China, different interpretations") and opposition to Taiwan's independence, and he also acknowledged that withdrawal of missiles would be meaningless since they are mobile. At the end of July 2010, the PLA responded publicly for the first time to Taiwan's demand that the PLA withdraw missiles. However, the PLA said that the two sides of the strait would discuss *both* of their military deployments in discussions of setting up CBMs. Moreover, the PLA could retain the threat of force or coercion as a political tool to influence Taiwan.

Taiwan's expectation for cross-strait military CBMs has not been consistent and has remained politically sensitive, especially concerning controversial visits by retired generals and admirals to mainland China. Nonetheless, in March 2010, Taiwan's MND set up a new Office of Defense Studies (linked to the Integrated Assessment Office) also acting as the preparatory office for a think tank. It has studied military contacts with the PLA.

## Taiwan's Commitment to Self-Defense and Defense Budgets

Congress has oversight of the Administration's dialogue with Taiwan about its self-defense and military budgets. Congress also has discussed with Taiwan these responsibilities. Since 2002, some have expressed increasing concerns about Taiwan's commitment to its self-defense, lack of leadership and consensus on national defense, investments in defense transformation beyond requests for U.S. platforms, and limited contributions in international security. Some U.S. observers and officials have urged Taiwan's civilian and military leaders to place more urgent

---

[156] Author's discussions. Also: Shuai Hua-ming, "Taiwan-U.S.-PRC CBM: From LY and Long-term Cross-Strait Defense Security Observer's Perspective," October 2009. As an example of Steinberg's "encouragement" of CBMs raising expectations in Taiwan of a U.S. role that could or could not be met, Chen I-hsin, a professor in Taiwan at Tamkang University who is also a vice president at the Foundation on Asia-Pacific Peace Studies (a think tank with support from President Ma and other officials that is studying cross-strait CBMs) wrote "U.S. Roles in the Cross-Strait Relations and Taiwan's Democracy," a paper for the International Conference on Obama's New Policy – New Situation in Asia Pacific and the Future Development of Taiwan, October 31, 2009, Legislative Yuan, Taipei. On June 15, 2010, an advisor on defense policy in the KMT and retired vice admiral, Lan Ning-li, published an article in *Lien-ho Pao* to criticize the many groups of Taiwan's retired generals visiting the PRC as its "pawns" to push for CBMs.

[157] *Lien-Ho Pao* [United Daily News], Taipei, November 3, 2009.

---

priority on upgrading Taiwan's self-defense capability and to increase defense spending, while noting that Taiwan has planned an independent defense (since it cannot assume foreign help).[158]

The Pentagon's report on PRC Military Power submitted to Congress in 2002 said that reforms in Taiwan's military were needed to achieve a joint service capability to meet the growing challenge from the PLA's modernizing air, naval, and missile forces, but warned that "the defense budget's steady decline as a percentage of total government spending will challenge Taiwan's force modernization." The Pentagon's report issued in 2003 further stressed that the relative decline in Taiwan's defense budget "increasingly" will challenge its force modernization. The Defense Secretary's report on the PLA submitted to Congress in 2011 critiqued (for the first time since 2007) that Taiwan's "budget shortfalls" challenged efforts to professionalize the military, that Taiwan's relatively modest defense spending failed to keep pace with the PRC's ambitious military developments, and that increased costs to attract volunteer, professional personnel could divert funds from arms acquisitions as well as near-term training and readiness, even with "eroding" defenses.[159] In answers provided for the Senate Armed Services Committee's hearing on February 9, 2012, on his nomination to be PACOM Commander, Admiral Samuel Locklear III replied to the committee's question on whether Taiwan is investing appropriately in its defense:

> Taiwan must ensure that it adequately resources its defense programs and defense transformation, to include looking at increasing its defense budget. I believe the best way to encourage Taiwan to invest more in its military is to send strong and consistent messages from the U.S. Government to Taiwan.

Meanwhile, the PRC has significantly increased military budgets, budgets that the Defense Department has assessed as markedly understating actual defense-related expenditures (by excluding funds for weapons development, foreign arms purchases, etc.). Still, the PRC's defense budget can be used as one indicator of the priority placed on the PLA's modernization. China contends that the defense budget is coordinated with economic development and accounts for only 1.3% of GDP. While that has been the case since 2001, China's rapid economic expansion has provided significantly greater resources for the PLA. China's defense budget has doubled every four or five years. The PRC's announced defense budgets have provided a sustained trend of mostly double-digit percentage increases in real terms since 1997 (after the Taiwan Strait Crisis of 1995-1996), except for 2004, 2009, and 2012. In March 2011, the PRC announced the 2011 defense budget at $91.5 billion. The Director of the Defense Intelligence Agency testified to the Senate Armed Services Committee on February 16, 2012, that China's total military spending could be estimated at as much as $183 billion in 2011. That estimate was double the budget. In March 2012, China announced a 2012 defense budget of $106.4 billion.

In Taiwan, some legislators argued in various ways that Taiwan's defense spending was sufficiently significant, that the legislature in a democracy has the right to scrutinize the defense

---

[158] Peter Brookes, "The Challenges and Imperatives in Taiwan's Defense," Heritage Lectures, January 9, 2003; John Tkacik, "Taiwan Must Get Serious About Defense," *Defense News*, January 27, 2003; John Tkacik, "Taiwan Must Grasp on True Defense Needs," *Defense News*, December 1, 2003; Wendell Minnick, "Taiwan Procurement in Shambles," *Defense News*, March 19, 2007; Randall Schriver, "Defense: Time to Take Ownership," *Taipei Times*, April 4, 2007; Ted Galen Carpenter, "Taiwan's Free Ride on U.S. Defense," *Wall Street Journal*, April 23, 2007; AEI and Project 2049 Institute (Taiwan Policy Working Group), "Deter, Defend, Repel, and Partner," July 2009; *Wall Street Journal* editorial, "In Taiwan's Defense," November 17, 2010.

[159] Secretary of Defense, "Annual Report on the Military Power of the People's Republic of China," July 12, 2002; "Report on PRC Military Power," July 30, 2003; "Military and Security Developments Involving the People's Republic of China, 2011," August 24, 2011.

---

budget, that economic challenges constrained defense spending, and that Taiwan did not need U.S. weapons in an accommodation with the PRC. The U.S. approvals of significant arms sales in 2001 came in the one year of negative real change in Taiwan's GDP (-2.2%). Also, Taiwan's officials and legislators pointed out that Taiwan had funded defense out of separate Special Budgets in addition to the regular (annual) defense budgets. Taiwan's Special Budgets for defense in 1994-2003 totaled US$22.6 billion and funded procurement of fighter aircraft and military housing construction. In 2003, anti-American attacks in Taiwan targeted perceived U.S. "pressure," "extortion," "sucker's arms deals," and "arms dealers' profits."[160]

In June 2003, Deputy Defense Minister Lin Chong-pin and a Defense Committee delegation led by Legislative Yuan President Wang Jin-pyng visited Washington to reassure the Administration and Congress that Taiwan remained committed to its self-defense.[161] A former official in the Pentagon involved in arms sales wrote in 2006 that the impasse over Taiwan's defense spending did not symbolize a lack of commitment to self-defense. Mark Stokes contended that the Bush Administration's policy on arms sales to Taiwan was right, but it came at the wrong time.[162]

Taiwan's regular defense budget for **2004** was about US$7.8 billion, which accounted for 2.4% of GDP and 16.7% of the total government budget, as compared with 3.8% of GDP and 24.3% of total spending in 1994. (See **Table 1**.) These relative declines took place even as the Pentagon warned of an increased threat posed by the PLA to Taiwan, U.S. support for Taiwan increased after the 1995-1996 crisis, and the PLA obtained higher budgets. For **2005**, Taiwan's Defense Ministry requested a budget of NT$260.7 billion, a *reduction* of NT$3.1 billion from that in 2004, and the final 2005 defense budget was NT$258.5 billion (about US$8.0 billion).[163]

In August 2005, the Defense Ministry requested a budget for **2006** of NT$265.7 billion, an increase of NT$7.2 billion from 2005. However, that budget included an initial request to buy PAC-3 missile defense units, after the Ministry lowered the Special Budget by removing funds for PAC-3. Minister of Defense Lee Jye acknowledged a major "crowding out" impact on the 2006 budget resulting from adding the PAC-3 request to the annual budget. He lamented that he had to cut out 53 new programs that would have invested in combat strength.[164] On January 12, 2006, the legislature voted to cut NT$11.2 billion (US$348 million) from the annual defense budget for 2006 (funds that would have been supplementary funds to support procurement of PAC-3 missile defense, P-3C aircraft, and submarines) and did not direct those funds to be used for munitions, training, or other defense needs. Taiwan's final 2006 defense budget was NT$252.5 billion (about US$7.8 billion), a *reduction* of NT$6 billion from the previous year. Meanwhile, the Minister of Defense requested a Supplemental Budget for the 2006 defense budget partly to procure U.S. submarines, P-3C ASW aircraft, and PAC-2 missile defense upgrades, given the lack of legislative approval for the requested Special Budget. In March 2006, the Defense Ministry requested a 2006 Supplemental Budget totaling NT$13.7 billion (US$420 million) for 74 defense programs, including NT$5.6 billion (US$172 million) for the three weapon systems, but the Cabinet did not agree with it.

---

[160] *United Daily News*, April 21, 2003; *China Times*, May 8, 2003, and August 18, 2003.

[161] Meeting at CRS with Lin Chong-pin and congressional staff, June 5, 2003; Luncheon at the Heritage Foundation with Taiwan's legislative delegation led by Wang Jin-pyng, June 24, 2003; TECRO, *Taipei Update*, July 22, 2003.

[162] Mark Stokes, "Taiwan's Security: Beyond the Special Budget," AEI, March 27, 2006.

[163] Consultations in Taipei and Washington; and FBIS report, October 22, 2004.

[164] *Central News Agency*, Taipei, August 30, 2005.

With general U.S. support, Taiwan's leaders stated a goal of reversing the declining spending trends and increasing the defense budget to **3% of GDP**. However, Taiwan has failed to reach this goal. In May 2005, Taiwan's Defense Minister Lee Jye requested that the defense budget increase from 2.4% of GDP to 3.0% of GDP in the next five years.[165] President Chen Shui-bian announced on September 12, 2005, the goal of increasing the defense budget to 3% of GDP by 2008, and this goal was stated in Taiwan's first National Security Report issued by President Chen in May 2006. In reaction to the report, the State Department issued a statement on May 19, 2006, to stress that the United States encouraged "Taiwan to boost its defense spending, concentrating in particular on immediate challenges of hardening and sustainability." Under DPP President Chen, Taiwan increased its defense budgets in 2007 and 2008. After the KMT's Ma Ying-jeou became president in May 2008, he retained the goal of defense budgets at 3% of GDP, a commitment reaffirmed in Taiwan's Quadrennial Defense Review (QDR) of March 2009 and the National Defense Report of October 2009. The QDR also declared an urgent imperative to participate more in regional security. However, President Ma cut Taiwan's defense budgets in 2009, 2010, and 2011, before providing an increase in 2012.

**Table 1. Taiwan's Defense Budgets**

| Fiscal year | Military budget (NT$ bil.) | Military budget (US$ bil.) | % of GDP | % of total government spending |
|---|---|---|---|---|
| 1994 | 258.5 | 9.8 | 3.8 | 24.3 |
| 1995 | 252.3 | 9.5 | 3.5 | 24.5 |
| 1996 | 258.3 | 9.5 | 3.4 | 22.8 |
| 1997 | 268.8 | 9.4 | 3.3 | 22.5 |
| 1998 | 274.8 | 8.2 | 3.2 | 22.4 |
| 1999 | 284.5 | 8.8 | 3.2 | 21.6 |
| 2000 | 402.9 | 12.9 | 2.9 | 17.4 |
| 2001 | 269.8 | 8.0 | 2.9 | 16.5 |
| 2002 | 260.4 | 7.5 | 2.7 | 16.4 |
| 2003 | 257.2 | 7.6 | 2.6 | 15.5 |
| 2004 | 261.9 | 7.8 | 2.4 | 16.7 |
| 2005 | 258.5 | 8.0 | 2.3 | 16.1 |
| 2006 | 252.5 | 7.8 | 2.1 | 16.1 |
| 2007 | 304.9 | 9.2 | 2.4 | 18.7 |
| 2008 | 341.1 | 10.5 | 2.5 | 20.2 |
| 2009 | 318.7 | 9.6 | 2.7 | 17.6 |
| 2010 | 297.4 | 9.3 | 2.2 | 17.3 |
| 2011 | 294.6 | 10.2 | 2.1 | 16.5 |
| 2012 | 317.3 | 10.6 | 2.2 | 16.4 |

---

[165] *Taipei Times*, May 24, 2005.

**Notes:** This table was compiled using data on the regular, annual defense budgets provided by the ROC's Ministry of National Defense, author's consultation, news reports, and data on GDP and exchange rates reported by Global Insight. The local currency is the New Taiwan Dollar (NT$). The FY2000 budget covered the 18-month period from July 1999 to December 2000. Taiwan also has separate funding for indirect defense-related spending (e.g., for retired veterans, military construction, etc.).

## Special Budget Proposed in 2004

In 2002, Taiwan's Ministry of National Defense said that it needed the legislature to approve NT$700 billion (about US$21 billion) over the next 10 years for arms procurement.[166] Taiwan's Defense Ministry has considered a Special Budget of $15 billion-$20 billion to procure the PAC-3 missile defense system, submarines, and P-3 ASW aircraft over 10-15 years. As discussed above, in 2003, Taiwan's military received the U.S. cost estimate for new submarines as well as price and availability data for PAC-3 missile defense systems and refurbished P-3C planes. In May 2003, Minister of Defense Tang Yiau-ming sent a letter to U.S. Deputy Secretary of Defense Wolfowitz, saying that Taiwan planned to submit a Special Budget to the legislature to procure the three weapon systems. However, Tang allegedly doubted the Special Budget would pass, while looking to the regular defense budget to fund items of priority to the Army.[167]

As Taiwan considered a Special Budget, the Pentagon urged a decision. In April 2004, Assistant Secretary of Defense for International Security Affairs Peter Rodman testified to Congress that "we have made clear to our friends on Taiwan that we expect them to reverse this budget decline. Though our commitments to Taiwan are enduring, the American people and both the Executive Branch and Congress expect the people of Taiwan to make their own appropriate commitment to their freedom and security." Rodman also stressed that "we expect Taiwan to go forward with its plan to pass a Special Budget *this summer* to fund essential missile defense and anti-submarine warfare systems and programs" [emphasis added].[168] On May 29, 2004, the Pentagon issued a report to Congress on PRC Military Power, stressing that "the principal indicator of Taiwan's commitment to addressing its shortfalls will be the fate of its annual defense budget" and that "the island's apparent lack of political consensus over addressing [its military challenges] with substantially increased defense spending is undoubtedly seen as an encouraging trend in Beijing."

On May 21, 2004, Taiwan's Defense Minister Lee Jye—a retired Naval Admiral personally committed to procuring new submarines—submitted to the Executive Yuan (Cabinet) a request for a Special Budget for defense totaling about US$20 billion.[169] On June 2, the Executive Yuan, controlled by the ruling Democratic Progressive Party (DPP), then passed a Special Budget of NT$610.8 billion (about US$18.2 billion), with about $4.3 billion for PAC-3 missile defense systems, $12.3 billion for submarines, and $1.6 billion for P-3 aircraft.[170] Taiwan's legislators have had the options of procuring all three systems, procuring one or two items, alternatives, or none. However, Taiwan's priorities remained unclear.

---

[166] *Chung-Kuo Shih-Pao [China Times]* (Taipei), May 17, 2002; *Taiwan Defense Review*, August 30, 2002.

[167] U.S.-Taiwan Business Council, "Defense and Security Report," 3rd Quarter 2005.

[168] Statement before the House International Relations Committee, hearing on "The Taiwan Relations Act: the Next 25 Years," April 21, 2004.

[169] *Central News Agency*, Taipei, May 26, 2004; *China Times*, Taipei, May 27, 2004.

[170] *Central News Agency*, Taipei, June 2, 2004.

---

## Taiwan's 2004 Legislative Delegation

The Special Budget was not passed in 2004, although the United States urged passage and welcomed the LY's president, Wang Jin-pyng of the KMT, who led a multi-party legislative delegation to the United States on June 17-27, 2004, to gain direct information on the weapons systems. The LY delegation visited Pearl Harbor Naval Base, HI; Washington, DC; and Fort Bliss, TX. Under Wang's leadership, legislators from different political parties reached a preliminary consensus in support of the Special Budget during their visit to Washington, where they met with Members of Congress and defense officials. They said they would seek a new cost estimate for the submarines, with the options of a construction or maintenance role for Taiwan's shipbuilding industry and delivery in 10 (not 15) years (after Deputy Secretary of Defense Wolfowitz personally expressed to the delegation U.S. opposition to Taiwan's more expensive proposal to build submarines domestically); and that they would consider splitting up the Special Budget to approve funds for the P-3C aircraft and PAC-3 missile defense systems, ahead of considering the subs.[171]

However, politicians made the Special Budget into a controversial political issue in gearing up for legislative elections on December 11, 2004. Opposition parties of the "blue coalition," the Kuomintang (KMT) and People First Party (PFP), called for drastic cuts in the Special Budget and retained their majority in the LY.

## U.S. Frustrations and Shifts

In April 2004, Assistant Secretary of Defense for International Security Affairs Peter Rodman told Congress that the Pentagon believed Taiwan's military needed to improve readiness, planning, and interoperability among its services.[172] In a speech in October 2004, Deputy Under Secretary of Defense Richard Lawless urged Taiwan's legislature to "vote in favor of Taiwan's national security."[173] In a strong tone, he warned that the Special Budget was a "litmus test" of Taiwan's commitment to its self-defense and that "inability" to pass the Special Budget would have "serious long-term consequences" (for foreign support, further intimidation from Beijing, and perceptions of Taiwan as a "liability"). Shifting the U.S. stress, Lawless called for Taiwan to expand its efforts from national defense to national security, and to pay attention to countering coercion, crisis management, and critical infrastructure protection (CIP) (of national command centers, telecommunications, energy, water, media, computer networks, etc.). Raising frustrations in the Bush Administration and Congress that Taiwan was not placing priority on self-defense, it became increasingly doubtful in 2005 that the LY would vote on the Special Budget and fund it at the full level, even if it would be considered. Meanwhile, the United States had increased concerns about and shifted focus to the regular defense budget and other questions about Taiwan's self-defense.

---

[171] Discussion with CRS and Congress on June 22, 2004; *United Daily News*, June 23, 2004.

[172] Testimony before the House International Relations Committee, hearing on "The Taiwan Relations Act: The Next 25 Years," April 21, 2004.

[173] Richard Lawless, Deputy Under Secretary of Defense for Asian and Pacific Affairs, Keynote Address, U.S.-Taiwan Defense Industry Conference, U.S.-Taiwan Business Council, October 4, 2004, Scottsdale, AZ. One of the ROC's Deputy Ministers of Defense, General Huoh Shou-Yeh, attended the conference.

---

## Cutting the Special Budget in 2005

In January 2005, President Chen Shui-bian told visiting Representative Tom Lantos that PFP Chairman James Soong changed his position on the Special Budget after visiting Washington where he met with Deputy Under Secretary of Defense Richard Lawless and Deputy Assistant Secretary of State Randy Schriver.[174] The following month, Lawless warned that Taiwan's failure to approve the Special Budget signaled that it lacked seriousness about its own security, raising questions about whether U.S. support has been necessary or not.[175] In February 2005, the Defense Ministry announced that the Special Budget's figure dropped to NT$590 billion (after appreciation of the NT dollar relative to the U.S. dollar) and that the request would be reduced to NT$480 billion (US$15.5 billion) (after removing certain costs, including an estimated US$2.3 billion associated with producing submarines domestically in Taiwan).[176] The reduced figure also factored in moving some infrastructure costs to the annual defense budget, but that budget has faced cuts. The Cabinet approved the new request on March 16 and submitted it to the LY.[177] Two days earlier, the PRC's National People's Congress adopted its "Anti-Secession Law," warning that the government in Beijing "may" use force against Taiwan.

However, Chen and Soong issued a "Ten-Point Consensus" on February 24, 2005, that did not mention the Special Budget. Indeed, the PFP raised another objection, saying that the major items should be funded out of the annual defense budget instead of a Special Budget.[178] The Defense Ministry began to consider asking for funds for the PAC-3 missile defense systems out of the annual defense budget, with submarines as the top priority rather than missile defense stressed by the Bush Administration.[179] In April-May 2005, the chairmen of the opposition parties, KMT's Lien Chan and PFP's James Soong, made historic visits of reconciliation to mainland China, meeting with Hu Jintao, Communist Party General-Secretary, Central Military Commission Chairman, and PRC President. These visits to the PRC further dampened prospects that the Special Budget would be passed.

## Congressional Appeals

On May 24, 2005, the LY's Procedure Committee failed to place the Special Budget on the legislative calendar, blocking consideration before the session's end on May 31. On May 27, Representative Rob Simmons and 32 other House Members wrote to KMT chairman Lien Chan, urging him to help expedite passage of the Special Budget in May. They warned that "failure to pass the special budget has raised concerns in the United States about Taiwan's ability to defend itself against potential aggression."[180] However, Lien responded in a three-page letter by making partisan attacks on the DPP and President Chen Shui-bian, and criticisms of the Special Budget although the KMT used special budgets in the 1990s.[181] Moreover, KMT and PFP members of the

---

[174] *Agence France Presse*, Hong Kong, January 17, 2005. The author also confirmed Soong's meeting with Lawless with the KMT/PFP's representative in D.C.

[175] *Taipei Times*, February 26, 2005; Lawless gave a speech that was not publicly released, apparently at a meeting in Washington of the U.S.-Taiwan Business Council.

[176] *Taipei Times*, February 16, 2005; February 23, 2005.

[177] *Ettoday*, Taipei, March 16, 2005.

[178] *Lien-ho Pao [United Daily News]*, Taipei, March 21, 2005.

[179] *Tzu-yu Shih-pao [Liberty Times]*, Taipei, March 21, 2005; *China Post*, March 22, 2005.

[180] Representative Rob Simmons, et al., letter to Chairman Lien Chan, Kuomintang, May 27, 2005.

[181] Lien Chan, Chairman of the KMT, letter to Rep. Simmons, et al., June 8, 2005.

---

LY's Defense Committee refused to attend a luncheon on June 9 with the top U.S. representative, AIT's Director Doug Paal, while his strained relationship with the DPP apparently required Deputy Director Dave Keegan to host the DPP lawmakers who showed up to discuss the arms sales.[182] There was no special session in the summer as the ruling DPP requested. On July 16, 2005, the KMT overwhelmingly elected Ma Ying-jeou (Taipei's Mayor) instead of Wang Jin-pyng (LY's President) to replace Lien Chan as KMT Chairman, prompting some to ask whether Ma would show leadership in considering the Special Budget. However, he focused on the city and county elections on December 3, 2005, when the KMT won 14 out of 23 seats.

On August 1, 2005, three co-chairs of the House Taiwan Caucus wrote to Ma Ying-jeou as the new KMT chairman. They urged him to "lead efforts in Taipei to ensure that the Legislative Yuan quickly passes a special arms procurement package or increases its annual defense spending." They also invited Ma to visit Washington.[183] However, Ma responded as the Mayor of Taipei on August 18 (one day before becoming KMT Chairman), by blaming the DPP administration for "procrastinating for three years," "negligence," and "lack of leadership," with no mention of Wang Jin-pyng's LY delegation in June 2004. Ma promised to focus his attention on the issue and to "work closely with the KMT caucus" in the LY after taking over the KMT chairmanship. He also declined to visit in September, writing that the LY will "address tough bills like the arms procurement bill."[184] However, after PFP Chairman James Soong met with Ma on September 7, he announced that the KMT and PFP party caucuses will continue to "consult each other" on whether to advance the Special Budget for consideration in the LY.[185] Meanwhile, Ma set up a KMT task force to study the arms issue, and there have been questions about whether the KMT would support certain arms purchases and incur rising differences with its weakening coalition partner, the PFP, after the December 2005 elections.

Before the LY's session began on September 13, 2005, the Defense Ministry submitted a new Special Budget to cover submarines and P-3C aircraft, moving the request for PAC-3 missile defense to the regular budget (so that the Special Budget was about half of the original amount). LY President Wang Jin-pyng of the KMT acknowledged the reduction as a goodwill gesture and said that "it is time to address the issue."[186] On August 31, 2005, the Executive Yuan approved a Special Budget of NT\$340 billion (US\$10.3 billion), after removing NT\$140 billion (US\$4.2 billion) for PAC-3s. On September 28, 2005, the Defense Ministry issued details on its latest funding request for eight submarines: about NT\$288 billion in the Special Budget and NT\$10.1 billion in the regular budget for a total of about US\$9 billion.[187]

## Defense Department Warned of Limits to U.S. Help

When asked about the LY's delay in deciding to purchase U.S. weapons, Secretary of Defense Donald Rumsfeld said in August 2005 that under the TRA, the U.S. obligation was "to work with Taiwan" on security assistance, but it was up to Taiwan make its own decisions.[188] On September

---

[182] *Taipei Times*, June 10, 2005.

[183] Letter from Representatives Robert Wexler, Steve Chabot, and Sherrod Brown (without Dana Rohrabacher) to Ma Ying-jeou, KMT Chairman, August 1, 2005.

[184] Letter to the Taiwan Caucus from Ma Ying-jeou, Mayor of Taipei, August 18, 2005.

[185] *Chung-kuo Shih-pao [China times]*, Taipei, September 7, 2005.

[186] *Central News Agency*, Taipei, August 24, 2005; *Taipei Times*, August 25, 2005.

[187] *Tung-sen Hsin-wen Pao*, Taipei, September 28, 2005.

[188] Secretary of Defense Donald Rumsfeld, news briefing, August 23, 2005.

19, 2005, Deputy Under Secretary of Defense Richard Lawless issued another strong speech, this time directed at Taiwan's people and saying that he was not urging the passage of the Special Budget because it has become a political "distraction." Lawless applauded the goal of increasing the defense budget to 3% of GDP. He warned of the danger that "Taiwan's steadily declining defense budgets, and the resulting erosion in its own defense capabilities, also adversely affect the status quo," in addition to the PLA build-up. He expressed the U.S. expectation that Taiwan has the "collective will to invest in a viable defense to address a growing threat and be in a position to negotiate the future of cross-strait relations from a position of strength." He criticized the military for "short-changing itself on reserves of critical munitions" and inadequate "hardening" for defense. Lawless stressed that, under the TRA, Taiwan also has an obligation for its self-defense. He warned that

> the time of reckoning is upon us.... The U.S. ability to contribute to Taiwan's defense in a crisis is going to be measured against Taiwan's ability to resist, defend, and survive based on its own capabilities.... As the lone superpower, our interests are plentiful and our attention short. We cannot help defend you, if you cannot defend yourself.[189]

Separately, PACOM Commander, Admiral William Fallon, raised questions in press articles and interviews about his assessment of whether Taiwan should prioritize its limited defense resources on "defensive" weapons rather than submarines, given Taiwan's urgent need to effectively upgrade its self-defense. Admiral Fallon reportedly raised this question with Taiwan's Chief of General Staff, General Lee Tien-yu, who recently had visited Hawaii. Admiral Fallon also told the *United Daily News* his concern that if he was to be able to maintain the U.S. commitment to assist Taiwan's defense, then Taiwan should have a strong self-defense capability.[190] On October 26, 2005, eight Members, led by Representative Simmons, asked Admiral Fallon to explain his discussions with Taiwan on submarines. Admiral Fallon responded that he has not tried to discourage this purchase. He added, however, that PACOM has "strongly and consistently encouraged [Taiwan] to acquire capabilities that would have an immediate impact on [its] defense," and "while submarines would provide Taiwan with significant capabilities, a lengthy period of time would be needed to fulfill this long-term acquisition program."[191]

On October 29, 2005, at the transfer ceremony for the first two Kidd-class destroyers, Marine Brigadier General John Allen, Principal Director for Asian and Pacific Affairs in the Office of the Secretary of Defense, gave a speech, saying that "it is imperative that the people of Taiwan hold their leaders of all political parties accountable for reaching a consensus to increase defense spending," while it was not appropriate for the United States to tell Taiwan what "budgeting mechanism" to use. The U.S. role, he said, was to provide the "assistance necessary" to help Taiwan's strategy for stability, "but at the end of the day, it is Taiwan that must decide its fate."

In the first notification to Congress on arms sales to Taiwan since March 2004, the Defense Department in October 2005 put a new stress on the TRA's objective, which was to assist Taiwan to provide for its "own self-defense."

---

[189] Speech issued on September 19, 2005, in San Diego, CA, at the Defense Industry Conference of the U.S.-Taiwan Business Council, while Richard Lawless was delayed in Beijing at the Six-Party Talks on North Korea's nuclear weapons. Edward Ross, a DSCA official, delivered the speech for Richard Lawless.

[190] *Japan Times*, September 26, 2005 [reprinted in *Washington Times*, October 8, 2005]; *Liberty Times* [Chinese-language newspaper in Taipei], October 12, 2005, which named General Lee Tien-yu; *Associated Press*, October 14, 2005 [reprinted in *Taipei Times*, October 16, 2005]; and *Lien-Ho Pao* [*United Daily News* in Taipei], October 18, 2005.

[191] Letter to Representative Simmons from Admiral William Fallon, November 8, 2005.

Like Lawless, the Director of DSCA, Air Force Lt. Gen. Jeffrey Kohler, also highlighted Taiwan's inadequate attention to its stocks of air-defense missiles and other munitions as well as pending decisions on defense spending, in an interview in December 2005.[192]

At a hearing of the House Armed Services Committee on March 9, 2006, in response to Representative Rob Simmons' question about the submarine sale to Taiwan, Admiral William Fallon expressed the dilemma for PACOM regarding Taiwan. Fallon said that he was:

> in bit of a box here, because I'm committed to defend this country in the event of any military aggression should that occur from the PRC, and yet the history is that they have not been forthcoming in investing in their own defense.... What I'd like to see is some steps being made, some investment by Taiwan to actually acquire some of these capabilities and to boost their own readiness and ability to provide for their own defense.

### Special Budget Blocked in Legislature

On December 13, 2005, opposition lawmakers in the Procedures Committee voted for the 41st time to block the statute governing the Special Budget, keeping it from the LY's agenda since it was first introduced in 2004. However, at the Procedures Committee meeting on December 20, the DPP and its allied lawmakers called a vote at a moment when they had a majority, and the committee voted 12-5 to report the statute to the LY. On the eve of full LY consideration, the KMT and PFP chairmen, Ma Ying-jeou and James Soong, announced their joint opposition to a "wealthy fool's arms deal." The Defense Ministry said it will move the request for P-3s and reduce the Special Budget to one request of NT$299 billion (US$9 billion), about half of the original Special Budget, for subs. Meanwhile, Representatives Rob Simmons and Tom Tancredo issued statements, saying the Special Budget was "critical for the defense of Taiwan" and applauded its passage out of the Procedures Committee. Representative Simmons also said that "blocking this arms package tells the United States—correctly or not—that Taiwan's leadership is not serious about the security of its people or its freedom. The American People have come to the aid of foreign countries in the name of freedom many times in our history; but Americans will not in good conscience support countries that are unwilling to defend themselves."[193]

When the LY convened on December 23, 2005, to consider the Special Budget, KMT and PFP lawmakers proposed to end the meeting before debating the bill. Taiwan's lawmakers voted 113-100 to end the meeting 20 minutes after it began. This move effectively sent the bill on the Special Budget back to the Procedures Committee, which then voted as before to block its progress on December 27, 2005, January 3, and January 10, 2006, the 45th time that opposition lawmakers blocked the statute on the Special Defense Budget after its introduction in 2004.

### Waiting for Ma Ying-jeou's KMT Defense Policy

LY president Wang Jin-pyng (KMT) visited Washington on January 24-25, 2006, and promised a KMT policy on defense from Ma Ying-jeou, including on arms sales, in February or March. Unlike his visit in 2004, Wang's highest-level interlocutors in the Pentagon were Deputy Assistant Secretary of Defense Mary Beth Long and the Principal Director for Asian and Pacific Affairs, Brigadier General John Allen. There were no results from this visit.

---

[192] Jim Wolf, "Pentagon Official Says Taiwan Short on Weapons," *Reuters*, December 7, 2005.

[193] Rob Simmons, "U.S. Congressman Congratulates Taiwan on Defense Spending Bill Progress," December 21, 2005.

---

In February 2006, Representative Rob Simmons visited Taipei and suggested a lower cost for the submarine sale (perhaps $8 billion) and an interim step for Taiwan to procure a sub design (perhaps $225 million). Also in February, Representative Henry Hyde, chairman of the House International Relations Committee sent a letter to Ma, citing "deep concern" in Congress about the LY's failure in the past two years to pass the Special Budget and about significant cuts in other defense spending that would improve readiness. Hyde also wrote that Americans are left wondering whether Taiwan's legislators have the resolve to meet the challenges in providing for Taiwan's own defense.[194] In a March 7 letter, Ma responded to Representative Hyde by blaming the DPP administration and promising his own policy in the near future.

While the House Taiwan Caucus, in August 2005, had invited KMT chairman Ma Ying-jeou to visit, he scheduled a trip to Washington for March 22-23, 2006, while Congress was in recess. Ma failed on March 14 to gain his party's approval to issue a long-awaited policy on defense and arms procurement, despite his upcoming visit to Washington. Ma had no details on his defense priorities in meetings during his visit (with the private sector and the Bush Administration). While campaigning to be president, Ma issued a defense policy in September 2007 with a stance that supported purchases of U.S. weapons, including submarines.

## *2006 Supplemental Budget Instead of Special Budget*

When the LY reconvened on February 21, 2006, the Procedures Committee blocked the statute on the Special Budget for the 46th time. Thus, in a March 20 special report to the LY, Defense Minister Lee Jye decided to request procurement of subs and P-3s through supplemental funds in the regular 2006 defense budget (instead of the Special Budget): NT$200 million (about US$6 million) as "working fees" to study a sub procurement program and NT$1.7 billion (about US$52 million) for P-3C aircraft. The Defense Ministry then decided also to request supplemental funds of NT$3.7 billion (about US$113 million) for PAC-2 upgrades (not PAC-3 missiles). The supplemental request for the 2006 budget for these three weapon systems totaled NT$5.6 billion (US$172 million). This amount for the three programs was included in the minister's 2006 Supplemental Budget request of NT$13.7 billion (about US$420 million) for 74 programs.[195]

In March 2006, the Defense Ministry submitted its request to the Executive Yuan (EY), or Cabinet, which then approved on May 24 a Supplemental Budget for the 2006 defense budget of NT$6.3 billion (about US$194 million) with the three weapons requests plus NT$700 million for construction of an airstrip on Taiwan-controlled Taiping island (in the Spratly Islands in the South China Sea). The Supplemental Budget also needed to be approved by the LY, but its session ended on May 30 and KMT legislators, including Lin Yu-Fang, raised concerns, particularly about the supplemental budget's legal basis.[196] The LY decided on June 12 to hold a special session on June 13-30, but consideration of the Supplemental Budget for defense was not on the agenda that focused on trying to recall President Chen from office. On June 14, the EY approved a draft bill to govern the Supplemental Budget. The KMT demanded in mid-October 2006 that the DPP Administration withdraw the original Special Budget if the Supplemental Budget was to

---

[194] Letter from Henry Hyde to Ma Ying-jeou, Chairman of the KMT, February 15, 2006.

[195] *CNA*, March 20 and April 4, 2006; Special Report of the Ministry of Defense, March 20, 2006; and author's interviews in Taipei in April 2006.

[196] During consultations in Taipei in April 2006, Lin Yu-fang said that a Supplemental Budget request would be illegal, that the issue is not the budgeting mechanism but whether the three weapon systems should be procured, and that such requests could "crowd out" other funding needs of the army and air force or other ministries.

be considered. While the DPP agreed to this compromise, it fell apart when the KMT and PFP still voted on October 24 to oppose placing the 2006 supplemental request on the LY's agenda.

This outcome prompted the U.S. Representative in Taipei, Stephen Young, to call a press conference two days later, at which he strongly urged the LY to "pass a robust defense budget in this fall's legislative session." He pressed the legislators to "permit the supplemental budget to pass through the procedural committee and be taken to the floor of the legislature so that an open debate can begin."[197] However, his remarks stirred controversy in Taiwan's charged domestic political context. In defiance of this latest U.S. message, the opposition KMT and PFP legislators voted in the Procedures Committee on October 31 to block the Supplemental Budget. On December 26, 2006, after some opponents forgot to vote against the supplemental bill, it was passed out of the Procedures Committee. Three days later, the LY voted (194-162) to allow committee review of the draft bill governing the supplemental budget but returned the supplemental budget to the Procedures Committee.

## 2007 Defense Budget

Taiwan reversed the negative trend in the budget for the Ministry of National Defense (MND), with an increase in 2007. In August 2006, the Executive Yuan (EY), or Cabinet, approved a proposed **2007** defense budget of NT$323.5 billion (US$9.8 billion), an increase of NT$71 billion (US$2.2 billion).[198] A proposal to buy F-16C/D fighters made up NT$16.1 billion (US$488 million) of this increase.[199] Without a Special Budget or 2006 Supplemental Budget, the Bush Administration, U.S. industry, and Congress shifted the focus to whether the LY would approve the 2007 defense budget with a spending increase during what was considered its critical September 2006 to January 2007 session. At the U.S.-Taiwan defense industry conference in September 2006, the Defense Department declined even to issue a policy address to Taiwan, after making the effort in 2004 and 2005. The State Department's Director of the Taiwan office warned Taiwan's political figures from opposition and ruling parties that "leaders who aspire to represent the Taiwan people" to the United States should recognize that their decisions "right now on core national security issues" will have an impact on the future bilateral relationship. He also focused attention on how the LY will pass the 2007 defense budget specifically "this fall."[200]

On November 6, 2006, the LY's defense and budget committees jointly passed an amended 2007 defense budget. They approved requested funds to procure P-3C ASW planes and PAC-2 upgrades; deleted about US$347 million for PAC-3 missiles; and cut the request for the sub program from about US$139 million to US$6 million (for the LY's own "feasibility study" for subs). They also froze funds for F-16C/D fighters for five months (ending on May 31, 2007), pending U.S. provision of price and availability data. However, the LY session ended on January 19, 2007, without passing a government budget, including the 2007 defense budget, because of a separate political dispute. Finally, on June 15, 2007, the LY passed the 2007 Defense Budget, with about: $6 million to conduct a "feasibility study" on buying submarines (not a commitment to either design phase or submarines); $188 million for P-3C planes; $110 million for PAC-2 upgrades (and no funds for PAC-3 missiles); and $488 million for F-16C/D fighters (with funds

---

[197] AIT Director Stephen Young, press conference, Taipei, October 26, 2006.

[198] *CNA*, August 23, 2006.

[199] Author's consultations with MND officials, September 2006.

[200] Clifford Hart, speech to the U.S.-Taiwan Defense Industry Conference, September 12, 2006, Denver, CO.

---

frozen until October 31 pending U.S. approval). The final 2007 defense budget totaled NT$304.9 billion (US$9.2 billion), accounting for 2.4% of GDP. However, without U.S. data, the Defense Ministry lost the funding for F-16C/Ds in the 2007 defense budget.

## 2008 Defense Budget

Regarding the **2008** defense budget, the MND requested and the EY approved in August 2007 a budget of NT$349.5 billion (US$10.6 billion), an increase of 15%. However, on December 20, 2007, the LY approved the final 2008 defense budget that totaled NT$341.1 billion (US$10.5 billion), making up 2.5% of GDP. The budget included funds (but also froze some of the funds) for procurement of PAC-2 upgrades, PAC-3 missiles, P-3C planes, sub design phase, F-16C/D fighters, utility helicopters, and attack helicopters.

## 2009 Defense Budget

The Bush Administration advanced the process for the programs for the P-3C planes and PAC-2 upgrades by formally notifying Congress of the proposed sales in September and November 2007. However, Taiwan's military had unused budgeted funds to apply to 2009 with no progress (no presidential notifications to Congress) on several other arms programs and with the U.S. refusal to accept a request for F-16C/D fighters through August 2008, when Taiwan's EY submitted the proposed **2009** defense budget to the LY, with a *reduction* from the previous year's defense budget. While Taiwan explained that the cut was due to unused funds for arms procurement, Taiwan could have increased its defense budget for the new transition to all-volunteer personnel, training, ammunition stocks, and maintenance. The LY failed to pass the government's budget by the end of 2008 and held an ad hoc meeting on January 15, 2009. The LY passed the final 2009 defense budget with NT$318.7 billion (US$9.6 billion), a cut of 6.6%.

## 2010 Defense Budget

In July 2009, the EY approved a total budget for 2010 and submitted the budget request to the LY in late August. However, after Typhoon Morakot also in August caused devastating destruction and about 700 deaths, President Ma replaced Taiwan's Premier and Cabinet. The new Cabinet took office on September 10 and replaced the budget with a new one.

Taiwan's military faced budgetary pressures as it also faced the challenges of deterring the PLA's continuing buildup, securing support from President Ma for defense upgrades, and losing funds from appropriated defense budgets due to delays that Taiwan did not expect in U.S. arms sales programs. Taiwan's MND regretted that it saw budgetary uncertainty and US$1.7 billion canceled from its appropriations in 2007 to 2009 due to the lack of U.S. approvals for sales of the F-16C/D fighters, a submarine design, and Black Hawk utility helicopters. After issuing the 2009 National Defense Report with the priorities in force buildup of information and electronic warfare, missile defense, counter air, sea control, and homeland defense, on October 22, 2009, Defense Minister Kao Hua-chu submitted to the LY a **2010** defense budget of NT$300.1 billion. The portion for arms acquisitions dropped in part because of the ongoing U.S.-Taiwan discussions. On October 28, the LY's Foreign Affairs and National Defense Committee froze for three months (pending the minister's report) funds totaling about US$135 million for the pending procurement of a U.S. submarine design, F-16C/D fighters, and Javelin anti-tank missiles. Yet, there was concern that the United States could question the LY's resolve, while it remained committed to the procurement of U.S. arms. The LY was expressing its frustration and asserting its role to press the

MND and the Ma Administration to deal with Washington's price increases and perceived delayed decisions. The LY also pressed the MND to carry out bold transformations, focusing on training, reorganization, operations, etc. (not simply cutting personnel).[201] On January 12, 2010, the LY passed the 2010 defense budget with a 0.9% reduction in the minister's request, to NT$297.4 billion (US$9.3 billion). This cut of 6.7% from the 2009 budget was greater than the cut of 5.2% in the total government budget.

## 2011 Defense Budget

In mid-2010, Taiwan's EY projected about NT$300 billion (US$9.4 billion) in the defense budget in 2011 and the same amount in the following two years. In contrast, the MND argued that it required over the next few years about US$3 billion in addition to the EY's projected budgets. Without the additional funds, the MND was concerned that it would have to delay the transition to an all-volunteer force (requiring even more funds to pay professional personnel), cut operations and maintenance funds (that could reduce readiness), postpone or cancel some arms acquisitions (while keeping the commitment to fund U.S. arms acquisitions), further reduce the force, or seek a special budget. The policy to reach an all-volunteer force faced another challenge due to Taiwan's low birth rate (that fell to a record low in 2010). In August 2010, the MND submitted to the LY the **2011** budget of NT$297.2 billion. As proposed by the Ma Administration, the defense budget would drop slightly from that in 2010. Legislator Lin Yu-fang told reporters that NT$45 billion (US$1.4 billion) would fund U.S. arms acquisitions, including those programs awaiting U.S. approval (e.g., submarines, F-16C/Ds). Lin also said in December 2010 that the budget included about US$2.9 billion for Black Hawk helicopters. The budget constraint compelled the Ministry of Defense to propose in October that the payment and/or production schedules be extended for the Patriot and Black Hawk programs, but media reports raised confusion with a claim that Taiwan "deferred" the buys. The Defense Ministry also sought to be able to reallocate funds if not used for U.S. arms (due to the lack of U.S. approvals). In addition to having to return to the Treasury about US$1.7 billion in unspent funds in the 2007-2009 budgets (as discussed above), the Defense Ministry allocated in each of the 2010 and 2011 budgets about US$130 million for F-16C/Ds and a sub design. Further, a claim of economic constraint was belied by Taiwan's high real economic growth of 11% in 2010 and the passage of a special budget for 2011 for infrastructure of US$5.3 billion. In early 2011, the LY passed the final defense budget of NT$294.6 billion (US$10.2 billion), at 2.1% of GDP and 16.5% of the total budget. When asked about Taiwan's cuts in the defense budgets during his address to the United States on May 12, 2011, President Ma claimed that defense spending could not keep up with the rapid GDP growth.

## 2012 Defense Budget

President Ma finally raised the defense budget for 2012. In October 2011, the EY submitted to the LY the proposed defense budget for 2012 of NT$317.5 billion, an increase of 8% from the 2011 defense budget. In December, the LY passed the final budget of NT$317.3 billion (US$10.6 billion). However, the **2012** budget would be 2.2% of GDP (still short of the goal of 3%) and would drop slightly as a share of the total government budget (from 16.5% to 16.4%). Moreover, higher costs for personnel (more volunteers) would account for 49% of the defense budget, reducing the portions for operations and maintenance to 22% and new procurements to 27%. The

---

[201] Author's consultations; *Lien-ho Bao*, Taipei, October 29; *Kyodo*, November 4; *Central News Agency*, November 12, 2009. In 2009, Taiwan's officials expressed frustrations with the increases in the per unit cost for the Javelin missiles.

budget includes amounts for procurement of U.S. systems, including the F-16A/B upgrades (with the notification to Congress in September 2011), new F-16C/D fighters, and the design phase for submarines. Further, it remains to be seen whether increases will continue, since this budget increase of $755 million was boosted by the repayment of $875 million from Thales in a lawsuit over the commission involved in the French company's contract in 1991 to supply frigates.

## Visits by Generals/Admirals to Taiwan

As for senior-level contacts, the United States and Taiwan have held high-level defense-related meetings in the United States, as discussed above. U.S. policy previously restricted high-level military contacts but changed to welcome Taiwan's senior military officers and defense officials to visit the United States, shifting the question to their willingness to make the visits. At the same time, the State Department's policy has avoided sending to Taiwan U.S. flag and general officers or officials at or above the level of Deputy Assistant Secretary of Defense or State. For a hearing in 1999, Assistant Secretary of State Stanley Roth responded to a submitted question on this issue by writing that "following the 1994 policy review, the Administration authorized travel by high-level officials, including cabinet officers, from economic and technical agencies. However, restrictions remained at the same level for visitors from military or national security agencies at or above the position of Deputy Assistant Secretary and at the rank of one-star flag officer or above. This policy is based on the determination that visits of such officials would be inconsistent with maintaining an unofficial relationship."[202]

The State Department has issued "Guidelines on Relations with Taiwan" (applicable only to the Executive Branch) to restrict contacts with Taiwan, including official travel to Taiwan for State or Defense Department officials above the level of office director or for uniformed military personnel above the rank of O-6 (colonel, navy captain), without State's approval.[203] The Pentagon and some in Congress have sought to lift this restriction in order to advance U.S. interests in boosting Taiwan's deterrence capability and U.S. leverage in Taiwan. Senior-level exchanges could help to understand Taiwan's crisis-management and self-defense capabilities and limitations.[204] The TRA does not specify unofficial or official relations with Taiwan. Some have cited the NSC's record of sending senior officials to Taipei for clear and direct talks.[205] Also, after starting in 2003 as the Deputy Under Secretary of the Air Force for International Affairs, Bruce Lemkin traveled twice to Taiwan by 2009 to discuss the Surveillance Radar Program (SRP) and other programs.[206] Nonetheless, the NSC, State Department, and some in Congress have opposed ending the general rule to send senior military officers and defense officials to Taiwan as an unnecessary, ineffective change in a sensitive situation.

---

[202] Senate Foreign Relations Committee, hearing on "United States-Taiwan Relations: the 20th Anniversary of the Taiwan Relations Act," March 25, 1999.

[203] Department of State, "Guidelines on Relations with Taiwan," latest issue of March 4, 2011.

[204] Dan Blumenthal and Gary Schmitt (AEI), "A Strange Calculus," *Wall Street Journal*, August 21, 2006; Therese Shaheen (ex-AIT Chairwoman), "Why is the U.S. Ignoring Taiwan?" *Wall Street Journal*, June 14, 2007.

[205] The NSC has sent the Senior Director for Asian Affairs, including James Moriarty and Michael Green, to Taiwan. For example: *Far Eastern Economic Review*, May 20, 2004.

[206] U.S.-Taiwan Defense Industry Conference, Charlottesville, VA, September 27-29, 2009; Jim Wolf, "New Chinese Fighter Jet Expected by 2018: U.S. Intelligence," *Reuters*, May 21, 2010.

---

## Taiwan's Missile Program

Policy-makers have faced an issue of how to respond to Taiwan's programs for counter-strike missiles (ballistic and cruise missiles). Some officials in Taiwan and U.S. supporters have talked about missiles as a deterrent.[207] Some Americans have viewed Taiwan's missile defense strategy with recognition of the tactical utility of missiles (including in U.S. military doctrine[208]) and as inherently defensive against the PRC's missile and other threats. They also have considered Taiwan's efforts in self-defense as its own decisions. Other officials and observers have raised a question of conformity to international missile nonproliferation standards of the Missile Technology Control Regime (MTCR). The MTCR is a set of voluntary guidelines in export controls to prevent primarily the transfer of missiles capable of delivering at least a 500 kg (1,100 lb) payload to at least 300 km (186 mi). However, Taiwan reportedly has developed missiles for its own defense, not for export. Taiwan has the options of unilaterally adhering to the MTCR and fielding missiles without U.S. involvement. Another argument has called the longer-range weapons unhelpful for stability and U.S. escalation control in a possible crisis or conflict.[209]

The Bush Administration objected to Taiwan's missile programs.[210] However, this objection raised an issue of whether the Administration contradicted its past position and undermined Taiwan's defense.[211] Another issue has concerned whether the refusal to consider Taiwan's request (first raised in 2006) for F-16C/D fighters undermined this concern about missiles. A third policy issue has questioned whether U.S. opposition should be stronger or whether U.S. concern should be limited to U.S. adherence to the MTCR, focusing on technology transfers.

At a press conference in October 2006, the U.S. Representative in Taipei, Stephen Young, said that U.S. policy helps Taiwan to have self-defense, "not to attack the mainland, because that was never in the cards and still isn't now, but to defend itself." By April 2007, the Administration became more concerned about a misperception of U.S. assistance for or approval of Taiwan's Hsiung-feng 2E (HF-2E) land-attack cruise missile (LACM) program. Also, U.S. officials reportedly linked Taiwan's planned deployment of such missiles to consideration of a request for F-16C/D fighters.[212] Right after Taiwan's Han Kuang exercise in April 2007, the new PACOM Commander, Admiral Timothy Keating, testified to Congress about the situation in the Taiwan Strait while expecting Dennis Blair's full briefing on the exercise. To clarify its intention for tactical utility of missiles, Taiwan issued a new name for the missile under development, called Tactical Shore-based Missile for Fire Suppression (TSMFS). Keating stressed "how emphatically we emphasize to [Taiwan] that [its] actions should be defensive in nature and not offensive."[213] Finally, because the Han Kuang military exercise included demonstration of the use of the LACM to Blair, a National Security Council official publicly stated,

---

[207] John Tkacik, "The Best Defense is a Good Offense," *Taipei Times*, February 14, 2007.

[208] See discussion in CRS Report RL30379, *Missile Defense Options for Japan, South Korea, and Taiwan: A Review of the Defense Department Report to Congress*, by Robert D. Shuey, Shirley A. Kan, and Mark Christofferson.

[209] Michael McDevitt, "For Taiwan, the Best Defense is not a Good Offense," PacNet #9, February 22, 2007.

[210] *Lien-ho Pao [United Daily News]*, Taipei, October 21, 2006, quoting unnamed U.S. officials.

[211] Rupert Hammond-Chambers, President of the U.S.-Taiwan Business Council, "Taiwan Goes It Alone," *Defense News*, and "Special Commentary," February 25, 2008.

[212] *Defense News*, July 16, 2007.

[213] Senate Armed Services Committee's hearing on April 24, 2007.

We think that developing defensive capabilities is the right thing to do. We think that offensive capabilities on either side of the Strait are destabilizing and, therefore, not in the interest of peace and stability. So when you ask me whether I am for offensive missiles, I'm not for offensive missiles on the Chinese side of the Strait, and I'm not for offensive missiles on the Taiwan side of the Strait. But appropriate defense capabilities are certainly the right of the people of Taiwan.[214]

AIT Director Stephen Young followed up at a news conference in Taipei in May 2007, stating that "there were claims that the United States Government approved of the use of long-range offensive missiles during the [Han Kuang military] exercise and that they even offered a name for these systems. I want to say categorically here, on behalf of the U.S. Government, that these stories are inaccurate." He added that "what we think Taiwan should be placing its emphasis on, is missile defense," citing the PAC-3 missile defense system.[215] In December 2007, Taiwan's LY approved about $117 million but froze $77 million for the HF-2E program in the final 2008 defense budget. Under KMT President Ma, Deputy Defense Minister Andrew Yang testified to the LY in March 2010 that Taiwan needed missiles for deterrence and maintenance of "peace through strength."[216] Taiwan reportedly budgeted in 2008-2010 to produce 300 HF-2E missiles with a range of 600-800 km (375-500 miles), a cut from 1,000 km, and KMT Legislator Lin Yu-fang said in August 2010 that the missiles (with unspecified number and payload) would be deployed to the Missile Command by the end of the year.[217]

## President's "Freezes" or Delays in Arms Sales Notifications

In 2008, congressional concerns and frustrations mounted about perceived delays in the President's notifications and briefings to Congress on eight pending arms sales as well as his refusal to accept Taiwan's request for F-16C/D fighters. As discussed above, **President Bush** changed policy in April 2001 to consider Taiwan's arms requests routinely on an as-needed basis, similar to acceptance of other foreign requests for security assistance. However, the President's refusal to accept a formal request from Taiwan for F-16C/D fighters since 2006 has raised the issues of whether the Administration violated or changed policy and did so without consultation with Congress. In October 2007, the House passed **H.Res. 676**, and Senator Lisa Murkowski wrote a letter to National Security Advisor Stephen Hadley.

In addition to the uncertainty of the Bush Administration's decision-making, there were also questions about any changes in the security strategy and defense policy of President Ma Ying-jeou, particularly given the past ambivalence of the KMT party. There were questions about the KMT's review of pending U.S. arms programs, reportedly including whether to pursue the submarine purchase.[218] After the inauguration of Taiwan's KMT President Ma on May 20, 2008, he promptly resumed a dialogue with the PRC on June 12-13, resulting in expanded charter flights and tourism across the Taiwan Strait in July. While the resumption of the cross-strait dialogue for the first time in a decade was welcomed, both the Ma and Bush Administrations were concerned about the timing of announcements on arms sales to Taiwan during the first round

---

[214] Dennis Wilder, Special Assistant to the President and Senior Director for East Asian Affairs, NSC, remarks at a Foreign Press Center Briefing, April 26, 2007.

[215] AIT Director Stephen Young, press conference, Taipei, May 3, 2007.

[216] *Tzu-yu Shih-Pao [Liberty Times]*, Taipei, March 30, 2010.

[217] *Chung-kuo Shih-Pao [China Times]*, Taipei, August 31, 2010.

[218] CRS Report RL34441, *Security Implications of Taiwan's Presidential Election of March 2008*, by Shirley A. Kan.

of the resumed dialogue, particularly concerns expressed by Ma's National Security Advisor Su Chi in discussion with a visiting Senate Foreign Relations Committee staffer in June.[219] Nonetheless, Taiwan later showed concern about the Bush Administration's delay in making progress on pending arms sales. On July 12, 2008, Ma finally clarified publicly that Taiwan still considered the U.S. arms programs as important and urgent, in spite of the cross-strait talks.[220] In the summer and fall of 2008, President Ma's military viewpoint reportedly was influenced by one U.S. article critical of the proposed arms sales programs, causing disarray and disputes between the Defense Ministry and National Security Council.[221] Visiting Washington on July 27-August 1, Wang Jin-pyng, President of the LY, said that U.S. officials told him that the Administration had not imposed a "freeze," continued to adhere to the TRA, and was working on the notifications. Taiwan's military was increasingly concerned about the potential loss of unspent budgeted funds for programs as it neared the end of the 2008 budget year.

Members of Congress suspected that President Bush effectively suspended arms sales to Taiwan in violation of the TRA and U.S. policy. Congress also was concerned about the lack of timely and complete information requested from the Administration, in disregard for the Congressional role. They feared that President Bush deferred to objections in Beijing or other considerations. Even before June, Deputy Secretary of State John Negroponte testified to Senator Lisa Murkowski at the Foreign Relations Committee on May 15, 2008, that after Taiwan's legislature approved funding of the weapons programs (which was in December 2007), the Administration did not take or plan to take subsequent steps in arms sales. Despite the lack of notifications to Congress on pending arms sales (after the last notification in November 2007), Assistant Secretary of Defense for Asian and Pacific Security Affairs James Shinn denied at a hearing that "we made a decision to put things in abeyance" in testimony on June 25.[222] (After the Bush Administration's notifications to Congress of arms sales to Taiwan in September and November 2007, the PRC protested by refusing to hold military exchanges, including an annual meeting on the Military Maritime Consultative Agreement (MMCA) scheduled for October 2007. The PRC also denied port visits at Hong Kong in November 2007 by U.S. Naval minesweepers in distress and by the aircraft carrier group led by the USS Kitty Hawk for Thanksgiving.)

On July 16, 2008, PACOM Commander Admiral Timothy Keating confirmed at a public event at the Heritage Foundation that the Administration's policy was to freeze arms sales to Taiwan. He reportedly confirmed discussions with PRC officials about their objections, raising a question about the Administration's violation of the TRA and Six Assurances. Moreover, Keating implied that arms sales would be "destabilizing" to the situation in the Taiwan Strait and that there was no pressing need for arms sales to Taiwan at this moment, even as he acknowledged a cross-strait military imbalance favoring the PRC. In contrast, former PACOM Commander Dennis Blair who just visited Taiwan in June said that Taiwan's military and civilian leaders understood the need to negotiate with the PRC from a position of strength and to maintain Taiwan's defense.[223] Also, former Bush Administration officials urged President Bush to keep his commitment on Taiwan.[224]

---

[219] *Washington Post*, June 12; *Defense News*, June 16; *Taipei Times*, June 20, 2008.

[220] *DPA*, July 12, 2008, and *Taiwan News*, July 13, 2008.

[221] William Murray, "Revisiting Taiwan's Defense Strategy," *Naval War College Review*, Summer 2008.

[222] House Armed Services Committee, hearing on China: Recent Security Developments, June 25, 2008.

[223] Wendell Minnick, "China Wields New Diplomatic Skills Against Taiwan," *Defense News*, July 7, 2008.

[224] Ed Ross, "Arming Taiwan," *Wall Street Journal Asia*, July 18, 2008; Dan Blumenthal, Aaron Friedberg, Randall Schriver, Ashley Tellis, "Bush Should Keep His Word on Taiwan," *Wall Street Journal*, July 19, 2008.

Some in Congress became concerned that the Administration suspended arms sales, but the Administration publicly denied a "freeze" or change in policy. The State Department responded in a letter to Representative Joe Courtney on July 17, 2008, arguing that the Administration was conducting an "inter-agency process" to consider Taiwan's requests for eight "highly complex" weapons programs, even though one program involved simply aircraft spare parts. In any case, the Bush Administration delayed sending notifications to Congress for eight approved, pending arms sales programs with a total value of $12-13 billion (for a sub design, Patriot PAC-3 missile defense systems, Apache helicopters, Blackhawk helicopters, E2-T airborne early warning aircraft upgrade, aircraft parts, Harpoon sub-launched anti-ship missiles, and Javelin anti-tank missiles).

As late as September 29, 2008, after the originally scheduled congressional adjournment on September 26, the Deputy Assistant Secretary of Defense for Asian and Pacific Security Affairs gave a speech at the U.S.-Taiwan defense industry conference, stating that he had "no news" on the long-awaited notifications on arms sales and that the Administration's "internal processes" were still continuing.[225] On **October 3**, the last day of congressional session that was extended to pass a bill to bail out banks during the financial crisis, President Bush finally notified Congress. A Pentagon spokesman said that the PLA suspended some military meetings and port visits, in "continued politicization" of contacts. (The PRC suspended such contacts in 2007, as discussed above.) The PRC also suspended bilateral talks to cooperate on weapons non-proliferation.[226]

However, President Bush submitted only six of the eight pending sales for a total value of $6.5 billion, or about half of the pending total. The Administration did not submit for congressional review the pending programs for Black Hawk helicopters or the submarine design. Moreover, the sale of PAC-3 missile defense systems was broken up, excluding three of seven firing units and about 50 missiles. Representative Ileana Ros-Lehtinen stated on the day of the formal notifications that they were in accordance with the TRA but criticized the President for not following the "letter and spirit" of the law and for keeping Congress "in the dark about U.S. arms sales policy toward Taiwan." She noted this "grave breach of Executive Branch cooperation with Congress." Also, Senator John McCain pointed out that the arms sales were "on hold for too long" and urged the Administration to reconsider its decision not to provide submarines or F-16 fighters.[227] In addition to freezing out Congress, the Bush Administration's long-awaited decision to submit the notifications raised more questions about arbitrary decision-making in addition to piling up the notifications for months (that were not programs in a so-called "package").

President Bush left confusion in the **process** for Taiwan to make requests for objective U.S. consideration of its defense needs and undermined his policy change of 2001 to depoliticize the decision-making. This situation raised the policy issue of whether to conduct a strategic review.

Despite concerns raised by President Bush's decision-making, **President Obama** repeated that process since 2008 to decide on submissions to Congress all at one time (no notifications for FMS programs after October 3, 2008, until his first notifications on **January 29, 2010**). On one day, he notified Congress of five programs (not a "package") with a total value of $6.4 billion that involved PAC-3 missile defense systems (a sale that was broken up into two parts with

---

[225] David Sedney, speech at the U.S.-Taiwan Defense Industry Conference held by the U.S.-Taiwan Business Council, Jacksonville, FL, September 29, 2008.

[226] *VOA* and *AP*, October 6, 2008; *Xinhua*, October 7, 2008; and author's consultations.

[227] Representative Ileana Ros-Lehtinen, ranking Republican, Foreign Affairs Committee, press release, October 3, 2008; and Senator John McCain, press release, October 7, 2008.

notification of one part in 2008), Black Hawk utility helicopters, Harpoon anti-ship training missiles, follow-on technical support for the Po Sheng joint command and control project, and Osprey-class minehunters (that Congress authorized for sale in P.L. 110-229). Like Bush, President Obama did not advance the submarine design program (the only one pending for notification to Congress stemming from decisions in 2001) and has not accepted Taiwan's formal request for F-16C/D fighters (pending for submission since 2006). Still, the Administration asserted on January 29 that it made no decision to rule in or rule out the submarine program and that it was still assessing Taiwan's requirement for new fighters.

The Obama Administration argued through 2009 that it did not "hold up" the notifications and was "reviewing" decisions in an "inter-agency process" and that at the U.S.-PRC summit in Beijing in November 2009, President Obama publicly reiterated the U.S. commitment to the TRA, signaling no change in the long-standing U.S. policy toward Taiwan. Nonetheless, the Presidential decisions raised questions about whether the process could return to routine reviews, whether Washington passed a watershed in arms sales, and whether Taipei will reduce defense acquisitions and budgets. Moreover, with the delays in decision-making since 2008 that were perceived by some in Washington, Taipei, and Beijing, the PRC harbored a rising expectation of compromise in U.S. policy on arms sales and issued more strident warnings than in the past.

The day after President Obama's five notifications on January 29, 2010, his Senior Director for East Asian Affairs at the National Security Council, Jeff Bader, met with the PRC ambassador and pointed out what the President authorized but also what was not authorized for sale to Taiwan. The ambassador said he noticed that point, which would mitigate the PRC's reaction.[228] The PRC threatened to respond in four ways: postpone "partial" military-to-military exchanges; postpone deputy ministerial level meetings on international security, arms control, and weapons nonproliferation; impose sanctions on U.S. defense firms involved in the arms sales to Taiwan; and react in interactions on international and regional problems. The immediate response was the PRC's postponement of Deputy Secretary of State James Steinberg's meetings in Beijing in February (that later took place in early March). The threat to U.S. firms was new in public but already existed and remained vague (with possible, partial impact on two companies with civilian business in the PRC, Boeing and General Electric) and risked backfiring on Beijing (in trade or other ties). Further, the PRC Embassy in Washington even called at least one U.S. defense firm's executive directly on a personal phone on a weekend in early February with an implied warning. The company countered that the PRC already had a "blacklist" against some U.S. firms, the embassy's contact was highly inappropriate, and the senior diplomat should direct the PRC's messages instead to the State Department. The firm then informed the State Department of the harassment against U.S. private executives.[229] In early June, the PRC did not welcome Defense Secretary Robert Gates when he proposed to visit while in Asia for the defense ministers' conference in Singapore (Shangri-la Dialogue). In his speech on June 5, Gates countered that U.S. arms sales to Taiwan are nothing new, do not support Taiwan's independence, and maintain peace and stability given China's "accelerating military buildup" that has focused on Taiwan. Still, while the PLA and others pointed to U.S. arms sales as the reason for the PLA's snub, another factor could have been the timing of a visit, right after South Korea announced on May 20 the finding that North Korea sank the South Korean naval ship Cheonan on March 26.

---

[228] Jeff Bader, *Obama and China's Rise* (Washington: Brookings Institution, 2012).

[229] Author's consultations in February and June 2010.

However, after President Obama's notifications in January 2010 and despite his statement and Gates's speech, the Administration held up at least three arms sales programs from early to summer of 2010.[230] Rather than the previous pending FMS programs that faced what critics called delays in notifications to Congress, these three programs involved Direct Commercial Sales (DCS) usually notified to Congress without controversy under Section 36(c) of the AECA. In July, Deputy Assistant Secretary of State David Shear strongly denied any "hesitancy" to sell arms to Taiwan. On August 10, 2010, the State Department notified Congress of one program that involved support for Taiwan's existing Hughes Air Defense Radar and Air Defense System (HADAR) and two programs to upgrade the GD-53 multimode radar on Taiwan's IDFs. Inexplicably, Taiwan's Ministry of Defense issued a statement to deny these were "arms sales."

After January 2010, President Obama did not notify Congress of major FMS until all on one day in September 2011. On September 21, 2011, the Administration submitted the formal notifications of three proposed programs totaling $5.9 billion: "retrofit" (or upgrade) of Taiwan's 145 F-16A/B fighters sold in 1992 ($5.3 billion); continuation of F-16 pilot training at Luke Air Force Base, AZ ($500 million); and aircraft spare parts ($52 million). The Administration argued that its arms sales to Taiwan were not negotiated with the PRC and already totaled $12.25 billion (together with the programs notified in January 2010), making up almost 80% of the total value of all the programs that President Bush notified in eight years (that totaled $15.6 billion), based on FMS in the table at the end of this report.

However, the programs for F-16 pilot training and aircraft spare parts were pending to continue long-standing cooperation. Also, after the State Department apparently suspended the process to provide price and availability data in September 2010, the F-16A/B program was expected to be notified to Congress since early 2011,[231] probably after PRC ruler Hu Jintao's visit in January 2011. Meanwhile, Taiwan's President Ma stepped up campaigning for his reelection in January 2012 and repeatedly requested U.S. arms as signs of political support. Indeed, one justification for the F-16A/B program was to support U.S. interests in political stability. The Administration decided to submit the long-awaited notifications and study on Taiwan's air power in September 2011. These actions came after Hu's and Defense Secretary Gates' visits in January, a PLA General's visit in May, the Chairman of the Joint Chiefs of Staff's visit in July, and Vice President Biden's visit in August, but before visits by Assistant Secretary of State Kurt Campbell, National Security Advisor Tom Donilon, and Deputy Secretary of State William Burns in October, and the G-20, APEC Summit, and East Asian Summit in November. Thus, despite the arms sales, officials continued to meet. After the announcement of arms sales, the PLA postponed visits by the PACOM Commander and the U.S. Army's band, a combined anti-piracy drill, and a combined medical rescue exercise with the PLA's hospital ship. Campbell and Acting Assistant Secretary of Defense Peter Lavoy proceeded to Beijing for the U.S.-PRC Consultations on the Asia-Pacific on October 11. By December 7, the PLA hosted Under Secretary of Defense for Policy Michele Flournoy for military-to-military Defense Consultative Talks (DCT). The PRC, again, did not make Taiwan face consequences for acquiring the American assistance.

---

[230] Rupert Hammond-Chambers (President of the U.S.-Taiwan Business Council), "Take China Out of the Driver's Seat on Taiwan," Opinion Asia column in *Wall Street Journal*, June 13, 2010. Also see *Defense News*, June 28, 2010.

[231] U.S.-Taiwan Business Council, "Defense & Security Report," Second Quarter 2011.

---

## Strategic Policy Review

During Taiwan's politically motivated impasse over funding for self-defense, a former Pentagon official warned in 2005 that if Taiwan did not pass the Special Budget and there were no expected improvements in defense, the United States would be more hesitant to approve future requests for weapons and possibly conduct a review of policy toward Taiwan.[232] Another former Bush Administration official contended in 2007 that U.S. policymakers should look at whether there was even a clear-eyed strategy for China that includes Taiwan's role.[233] After Taiwan passed arms procurement funds in 2007, the Bush Administration delayed progress on some arms sales in 2008, and the Obama Administration did not decide on major FMS in 2009, delaying notifications to Congress until January 2010. This situation raised a policy option of resurrecting the annual arms sales talks.[234] Another option would rectify President Bush's policy of 2001 to consider Taiwan's requests on an as-needed basis. U.S. policy could reassess arms sales in the context of Taiwan's joint defense requirements in a regional approach that includes addressing a rising China. An alternative would be to conduct a more serious and consequential defense dialogue, beyond the existing meetings whose effectiveness has come under question by some in Taiwan and the United States. Taiwan has lacked clear answers to some requests for weapons, while Taiwan has cut its defense budget. There have been rising concerns about the military imbalance in the Taiwan Strait. Taiwan could help with U.S. and international security concerns, in common interests. One option would be for a new annual "two-plus-two" strategic dialogue between officials from the Departments of Defense and State and their counterparts from Taiwan.[235]

Congress has a role in oversight of any reviews of policy toward Taiwan and could hold hearings even without the Administration's formal policy review. There has been no major policy review acknowledged to Congress since 1994. In September 1994, the Clinton Administration explicitly and publicly testified to Congress about a major **Taiwan Policy Review**.[236] Defense ties would likely be included in any policy reviews of how to enhance leverage over Taiwan and affect the cross-strait situation, including whether to limit defense ties, apply conditions, or strengthen ties. Policy promotes the U.S. objectives of assisting Taiwan's self-defense capability, preventing conflict, minimizing the chance of U.S. armed intervention, dispelling dangerous misperceptions, and promoting cross-strait dialogue. While U.S. objectives have been consistent, developments in China and Taiwan since the 1970s have required U.S. re-assessments and responses.

In late 2002, the Pentagon reportedly conducted a policy review of cooperation with Taiwan that examined whether its leaders have taken defense seriously, whether defense cooperation with Taiwan has been effective, and whether U.S. policy should change.[237] (The NSC, State Department, and AIT would have input into any review by the Administration of policy toward

---

[232] Interview with Mark Stokes, retired Air Force Lieutenant Colonel and Country Director in the Office of the Secretary of Defense, in *Taipei Times*, April 24, 2005.

[233] Randall Schriver, "In Search of a Strategy," *Taiwan Business Topics*, September 2007, AmCham, Taipei.

[234] Mark Stokes, "Taiwan Must Review Security Risks," *Taipei Times*, March 12, 2008. On the annual arms sales talks, see CRS Report RS20365, *Taiwan: Annual Arms Sales Process*, by Shirley A. Kan.

[235] Walter Lohman (Heritage Foundation) and Rupert Hammond-Chambers (U.S.-Taiwan Business Council), "Shore Up U.S.-Taiwan Relations Now As Two-China Tensions Have Abated," *Investor's Business Daily*, October 6, 2010.

[236] Assistant Secretary of State for East Asian and Pacific Affairs Winston Lord, "Taiwan Policy Review," before the Senate Foreign Relations Committee on September 27, 1994. See CRS Report RL30341, *China/Taiwan: Evolution of the "One China" Policy—Key Statements from Washington, Beijing, and Taipei*, by Shirley A. Kan.

[237] *Taiwan Defense Review*, January 18, 2003.

---

Taiwan.)[238] At the U.S.-Taiwan Business Council's conference on Taiwan's defense in February 2003, in San Antonio, TX, Deputy Assistant Secretary of Defense Richard Lawless told Taiwan's Vice Defense Minister Chen Chao-min and others that, while the President said that we will do whatever it takes to help Taiwan defend itself, Taiwan "should not view America's resolute commitment to peace and stability in the Taiwan Strait as a substitute for investing the necessary resources in its own defense." At the same occasion, Deputy Assistant Secretary of State Randall Schriver indicated a new proactive U.S. approach to Taiwan's defense modernization, pointing Taiwan to three priorities: missile defense, command and control, and ASW.

Taiwan's election in March 2004 brought the reelection of President Chen Shui-bian and his advocacy of a new constitution for Taiwan by 2008. In April 2004, the Defense and State Departments testified at a hearing on Taiwan of the **House International Relations Committee**, expressing a readjustment in the Bush Administration's policy toward Taiwan.[239] Assistant Secretary of State James Kelly clarified U.S. policy by stating:

- The United States "does not support" independence for Taiwan or unilateral moves that would change the status quo "as we define it" and opposes statements or actions from either side that would unilaterally alter Taiwan's "status."

- U.S. efforts at deterring PRC coercion "might fail" if Beijing ever becomes convinced Taiwan is embarked upon a course toward independence and permanent separation from China, and concludes that Taiwan must be stopped.

- It would be "irresponsible" of us or of Taiwan's leaders to treat the PRC's statements as "empty threats."

- The United States looks to President Chen to exercise the kind of responsible, democratic, and restrained leadership that will be necessary to ensure a peaceful and prosperous future for Taiwan.

- There are "limitations" with respect to what the United States will support as Taiwan considers possible changes to its constitution.

- We urge Beijing and Taipei to pursue dialogue "as soon as possible" through any available channels "without preconditions."

One policy issue has concerned the relative stress on cross-strait **dialogue vs. deterrence**. In his testimony, Assistant Secretary of State Kelly argued that a premise of arms sales to Taiwan has been that "a secure and self-confident Taiwan is a Taiwan that is more capable of engaging in political interaction and dialogue with the PRC, and we expect Taiwan will not interpret our support as a blank check to resist such dialogue." However, some observers questioned the continued validity of this premise. James Lilley, former ambassador in Beijing and representative in Taipei, warned in April 2004 that

> The implicit American premise was that a secure and stable Taiwan would be a more willing and successful partner in dealing with China. Judicious arms sales to Taiwan were part of this formula and in the past it has worked.... If elements of this broader formula are disregarded by the current Taiwan authorities, however, then the successful historic pattern has been broken. U.S. military support and arms sales cannot be used by Taiwan to move

---

[238] *The Nelson Report* (January 31, 2003) reported there was an interagency East Asia Policy Review.

[239] House International Relations Committee, "The Taiwan Relations Act: The Next 25 Years," April 21, 2004.

away from China—they were meant to make Taiwan feel secure enough to move toward accommodation with China. Our support should be conditional on upholding our successful pattern.[240]

Any policy review might be coordinated with **allies in Asia and Europe**, involving a regional strategy to deal with a rising China. While in Beijing in August 2004, Australian Foreign Minister Alexander Downer expressed doubts about whether any U.S. military help for Taiwan's defense against China would involve invoking Australia's defense treaty with the United States.[241] Nonetheless, in its Defense White Paper of 2009, Australia stated particular concern about the rise of China and about the Taiwan question as a source of potential miscalculation. In February 2005, Secretary of Defense Donald Rumsfeld and Secretary of State Condoleezza Rice with Japan's Ministers for Defense and Foreign Affairs issued a Joint Statement of the U.S.-Japan Security Consultative Committee ("2+2 statement"). They declared that a common strategic objective was to "encourage the peaceful resolution of issues concerning the Taiwan Strait through dialogue." China objected to the alliance's mere mention of Taiwan. In addition to Japan, Taiwan also lies in proximity to the Philippines, another U.S. ally. In December 2007, the Council of the European Union (EU) approved "Guidelines on the EU's Foreign and Security Policy in East Asia" that expressed concern about stability in the Taiwan Strait.

Greater cross-strait integration has raised concerns about the leakage of military technology, intelligence, and other **secrets** from Taiwan to mainland China. As supporters of Taiwan wrote in October 2006, "there is little sense in America's continued support of Taiwan's defenses if Taiwan has no intention of using them to deter attack by the Chinese. Washington is increasingly alarmed that Taiwan's politicians—wittingly or unwittingly—are shifting responsibility for their island's defense from Taipei to Beijing, thus jeopardizing the integrity of U.S. defense technology that has already been transferred to Taiwan."[242] Others have pointed out that Taiwan has its own concern about the control of military information and technology that could leak to the PRC and that the United States has transferred weapons to countries like Pakistan with close ties to the PLA.

A critical case of compromising Taiwan's intelligence and military, including the U.S.-origin Po Sheng C4 program, came to light on February 8, 2011, when Taiwan's military announced the detention on January 25 of Army Major General Lo Hsien-che for allegedly passing secrets to the PRC after PRC intelligence recruited him (while assigned in Thailand in 2002-2005). He could have continued to pass sensitive information after subsequent assignment at Army headquarters as director of the Communications and Electronic Information Department and promotion in 2008 to major general with even broader access to information on command and control. Lo was reported as Taiwan's highest-ranking alleged military spy for the PRC in decades and was not uncovered until 2010, with U.S. counter-intelligence involvement in investigations. In an interview with the *Washington Post*, Taiwan's President Ma acknowledged that this "very serious case" started in 2002 and, *after* its discovery in 2010, Taiwan's military started "stricter safeguards" and damage control. On July 25, 2011, a military court sentenced Lo to life in prison for spying for the enemy.

Taiwan was not the only compromise. Cases in the United States that concerned PRC espionage against Taiwan and U.S.-Taiwan weapons programs (including Po Sheng) involved Gregg Bergersen and James Fondren, Jr. Bergersen was a weapon systems policy analyst at the Defense

---

[240] James Lilley, "Strait Talk," *Wall Street Journal*, April 19, 2004.

[241] Catherine Armitage, "Downer Assures China on Taiwan," *The Australian*, August 18, 2004.

[242] Michael Needham and John Tkacik, "Grim Future for Taiwan's Defenses," Heritage Foundation, October 31, 2006.

Security Cooperation Agency (DSCA), the agency involved in arms sales, and was arrested in February 2008 and sentenced in July 2008 to 57 months in prison. Fondren was a civilian official in PACOM's Washington office and was sentenced in January 2010 to 36 months in prison.[243]

Still, there have been concerns about structural weaknesses in Taiwan that could allow for broad (beyond a need to know) and unquestioned access to secrets (particularly by general and flag officers or senior civilian officials), as compared to U.S. compartmentalized information, background security investigations, and routine procedures for safeguarding classified data and discussions. While it was possible that there was a coincidence that these cases involved the Po Sheng C4 program or that the PRC targeted Po Sheng, it was probable that PRC espionage has been aggressive and comprehensive in targeting the militaries of Taiwan, the United States, and other countries, which included Taiwan's C4 system. Moreover, in August 2011, Taiwan failed to detain a citizen who worked on arms programs in Taiwan (including Po Sheng), Ko-Suen Moo, who was arrested in 2005 and then jailed in the United States for trying to sell military parts (including an F-16 fighter engine) to the PRC. U.S. Immigration and Customs Enforcement (ICE) stated that it deported Moo to Taipei on August 17, 2011, and handed him over to local authorities. Despite the U.S. expectation of legal action, Taiwan's government "lost" Moo.[244]

In late February 2012, a news magazine in Taiwan reported that an Air Force Captain Chiang was detained in mid-January for allegedly leaking secrets to the PRC that involved a Regional Operations Control Center (ROCC). Taiwan's MND issued a statement on February 29 to confirm that he was turned over to prosecutors and to contend that it minimized any damage by tightening security after Lo Hsien-che's case. The military reportedly watched Chiang for four years. Nonetheless, this case raised questions as to why Taiwan did not announce the arrest until the media reported on it, whether the arrest was delayed until after the presidential election on January 14, and whether Taiwan briefed the U.S. side (with U.S. programs potentially harmed). A number of other cases in Taiwan's military of alleged spying for Beijing also have come to light.

In addition, after the KMT's Ma Ying-jeou became president in May 2008, there has been a question of whether Taiwan's pursuit of closer integration with the PRC—beyond détente—has an implication of Taiwan's **strategic reorientation** away from the United States and U.S. democratic allies like Japan and South Korea toward the PRC.[245] Indeed, on June 10, within weeks of President Ma's inauguration, a boat from Taiwan sank in the East China Sea after a collision with a coast guard ship from Japan near the disputed Senkaku islands (claimed as the Tiaoyutai islands in Taiwan and Diaoyu islands in the PRC). The situation escalated into a crisis between Taiwan and Japan. A KMT legislator, Lin Yu-fang, demanded that the Ministry of National Defense deploy one of the Kidd-class destroyers that the United States sold for Taiwan's self-defense to take legislators to the disputed maritime area. Not until a week later did President Ma call for a "peaceful resolution" and KMT legislators put off their plan to assert Taiwan's claims with a trip on a naval vessel. Then, from May to December 2009, President Ma met only twice with Japan's Representative to Taipei Masaki Saito, in a dispute over Saito's note of Japan's long-held stance that Taiwan's status remained unsettled. On May 20, 2010, when South Korea

---

[243] Taiwan's Ministry of National Defense, February 8, 2011; *Tzu-yu Shih-pao* [Liberty Times], February 9, 2011; *Chung-kuo Shih-pao* [China Times], February 10, 2011; *Washington Post*, February 17, 2011; *Taipei Times*, February 18, 2011; Department of Justice, releases, February 11, 2008, July 11, 2008, May 13, 2009, and January 22, 2010.

[244] ICE, "ICE Removes Taiwanese National Who Conspired to Export Sophisticated U.S. Military Equipment to China," August 18, 2011; *Taipei Times*, August 20 and 22, 2011. Yet, on June 30, 2011, Taiwan's prosecutors indicted Lee Teng-hui, who was president from 1988 to 2000, for allegedly diverting $7.8 million in diplomatic funds.

[245] CRS Report RL34441, *Security Implications of Taiwan's Presidential Election of March 2008*, by Shirley A. Kan.

issued findings that North Korea sank its naval ship (Cheonan) on March 26, killing 46 sailors, Taiwan issued a statement that raised questions in the United States and Asia about Taiwan's weak support for South Korea and whether Taiwan was out of alignment with the United States and allies. Later in 2010, Taiwan protested to Japan when it expanded slightly the Air Defense Identification Zone (ADIZ) to fully cover the airspace over Yonaguni island, though there was no impact on Taiwan. After U.S. enactment of the Comprehensive Iran Sanctions, Accountability, and Divestment Act (CISADA) of 2010 as **P.L. 111-195** on July 1, 2010, that followed U.N. Security Council Resolution 1929 of June against Iran's nuclear program, Taiwan did not announce its own sanctions against dealings with Iran's oil and gas industry. Other countries that imposed unilateral sanctions included Canada, Australia, the European Union, Japan, and South Korea. After North Korea attacked South Korea's Yeonpyeong island in November 2010, Taiwan's Executive Yuan (Cabinet) first targeted North Korea as well as South Korea for "self-restraint," but President Ma Ying-jeou followed the next day with a stronger condemnation of North Korea. After Japan's catastrophic earthquake, tsunami, and nuclear disaster in March 2011, President Ma led Taiwan to be the largest donor of official and private aid, including $3.5 million from the government, though Taiwan's military and coast guard did not offer assistance to Japan.

Despite a lack of consensus in Taiwan, its closer engagement with the PRC under KMT President Ma Ying-jeou since May 2008 raised an issue among some academics of whether to review U.S. policy. Related issues concern whether U.S. policy should "abandon" Taiwan and accommodate a rising China, whether Taiwan itself has accommodated China, and whether to seek alternative approaches to sustain stability.[246] One debate centered on the relative importance of a **"balance of power" versus "peace and stability"** in the U.S. objective. A better defined strategy to set clear objectives and improve mutual consensus might be needed. The dynamics of the closer cross-strait interactions have positive and negative implications for U.S. interests and influence.

For the hearing on January 13, 2009, on Hillary Clinton's nomination as Secretary of State, the Senate Foreign Relations Committee asked a question for the record about whether the Obama Administration would hold another Taiwan Policy Review, but she did not answer the question. Meanwhile, more narrowly than a review by the Administration, Admiral Robert Willard, Commander of PACOM in Honolulu, initiated in January 2010 reviews of approaches toward the PRC and toward Taiwan (among other concerns like North Korea) by "Strategic Focus Groups (SFGs)" under a Director of Strategic Synchronization.

With the suspected delays or freezes in notifications to Congress of arms sales, particularly since 2008, there has been an issue of whether the Administration has adhered to the TRA. In March

---

[246] See Robert Sutter's presentation at a conference at George Washington University on January 29, 2009; Nadia Tsao, "U.S. Urged to Review Taipei Policy," *Taipei Times*, January 31, 2009; Robert Sutter, "Cross-Strait Moderation and the United States – Policy Adjustments Needed," *PacNet Newsletter* #17, March 5, 2009; Richard Bush and Alan Romberg, "Cross-Strait Moderation and the United States—A Response to Robert Sutter," *PacNet Newsletter* 17A, March 12, 2009, Pacific Forum CSIS; and Robert Sutter, "Taiwan's Future: Narrowing Straits," *NBR Analysis*, May 2011. Also see controversial academic articles with a theme of what some called "abandoning" Taiwan in *Foreign Affairs* by Bruce Gilley, "Not So Dire Straits: How the Finlandization of Taiwan Benefits U.S. Security," January/February 2010; responses in May/June 2010; Charles Glaser, "Will China's Rise Lead to War? Why Realism Does Not Mean Pessimism," March/April 2011; responses by Daniel Blumenthal, "Rethinking U.S. Foreign Policy Towards Taiwan," *Foreign Policy*'s Shadow Government blog, March 2, 2011, and Shyu-tu Lee and Douglas Paal in *Foreign Affairs*, July/August 2011. Also see Joseph Prueher, Charles Freeman III, Timothy Keating, David Michael Lampton, James Shinn, et al., "A Way Ahead with China," University of Virginia, January 2011; Nancy Bernkopf Tucker and Bonnie Glaser, "Should the United States Abandon Taiwan?", *Washington Quarter*, Fall 2011; Michael Swaine, "China Taiwan, U.S.: Status Quo Challenged," *National Interest*, October 11, 2011.

2011, the U.S.-Taiwan Business Council, which represents U.S. defense and other companies, contended that the U.S. commitment to Taiwan's defense has weakened. The next month, William Bader, who was Chief of Staff of the Senate Foreign Relations Committee in 1978-1981 when Congress passed the TRA, argued that the George W. Bush and Obama Administrations "have shown little to no knowledge or real interest in the Taiwan Relations Act."[247]

A related question has concerned whether U.S. strategy considers Taiwan's security role more narrowly in the Taiwan Strait or more comprehensively in the Pacific or globally. A question, then, was whether Taiwan was included in the U.S. defense strategy that Defense Secretary Robert Gates wrote in 2010, when he called for "building partner capacity: helping other countries defend themselves or, if necessary, fight alongside U.S. forces by providing them with equipment, training, or other forms of security assistance."[248] Secretary Gates also addressed whether to review policy toward Taiwan, including on arms sales, when he visited the PRC in January 2011 and said to reporters that "clearly over time if the environment changed and if the relationship between the China and Taiwan continued to improve and the security environment for Taiwan changed, then perhaps that would create the conditions for reexamining all of this. But that would be an evolutionary and a long-term process."

# Major Congressional Action

### 112th Congress

On the eve of PRC ruler Hu Jintao's state visit to Washington in January 2011, the four Co-chairs of the House Taiwan Caucus and 23 Members of the Senate Taiwan Caucus wrote letters to President Obama, urging him to remain mindful of Taiwan's "vital security interests."[249] On April 13, Representative Robert Andrews introduced **H.Con.Res. 39**, *inter alia*, to express the sense of Congress that the President should sell F-16C/D fighters and upgrade Taiwan's F-16A/Bs.

Senator Richard Lugar, ranking Member of the Foreign Relations Committee, wrote to Secretary of State Hillary Clinton on April 1, 2011, stressing that arms sales to Taiwan has become an urgent matter and urging for a favorable decision on both sustainment of the F-16A/Bs and sales of new F-16C/Ds. Senator Lugar also called for meaningful consultation with the Committee. The State Department responded on April 14 that it has given "every consideration" to Taiwan's request to upgrade F-16A/Bs but failed to address why the Administration has not accepted or approved Taiwan's formal Letter of Request (LOR) for new F-16C/Ds. Senator Lugar sent another letter on May 5 to Secretaries Gates and Clinton, asking again for clarity on Taiwan's LOR for F-16C/Ds, stressing that opposition to a request for F-16C/D fighters would appear to be at odds with a consistent policy on Taiwan, and noting that Taiwan was designated a Major Non-NATO Ally and thus should be allowed to submit its requests for consideration. The Defense Secretary did not send his own response, and the State Department waited four months to respond, submitting a letter on September 14 (for both the Departments of Defense and State).

---

[247] U.S.-Taiwan Business Council, "The American Defense Commitment to Taiwan Continues to Deteriorate," March 1, 2011; William Bader, "U.S. Has Law that Governs Relations with Taiwan," *Financial Times*, April 7, 2011.

[248] Robert Gates, "Helping Others Defend Themselves," *Foreign Affairs*, May/June 2010.

[249] Letters to President Obama from Representatives Shelley Berkeley, Phil Gingrey, Gerald Connolly, and Mario Diaz-Balart, January 12, 2011; and 23 Senators led by Co-chairs Robert Menendez and James Inhofe, January 14, 2011.

---

At a hearing of the House Foreign Affairs Committee on May 12, 2011, the chair, Representative Ileana Ros-Lehtinen, asked whether China has a veto over U.S. arms sales and whether the State Department violated promises to consult with Congress and the requirement for the Javits Report. (§25 of the AECA requires a classified report to Congress on annual, eligible major arms sales.) Under Secretary of State for Arms Control and International Security Ellen Tauscher denied that China has a veto. Principal Deputy Under Secretary of Defense for Policy James Miller conceded that his department owed Congress another assessment on Taiwan's air defense.

On May 26, 45 Senators led by the Co-chairs of the Taiwan Caucus, Senators Menendez and Inhofe, wrote to President Obama, urging him to accept Taiwan's LOR for a sale of F-16C/D fighters. On June 13, Senator Lisa Murkowski sent a letter to President Obama, urging him to sell the fighters. As another congressional catalyst for decision-making, at the Heritage Foundation on June 29, Senator John Cornyn said that he spoke with Secretary of State Hillary Clinton the day before about his hold on the nomination of William Burns to be her Deputy Secretary as leverage to urge the Administration to submit a pending report on Taiwan's air defense and to accept (not necessarily approve) Taiwan's LOR for F-16C/Ds, and that she claimed the report remained in inter-agency review that would take three months or so more. Then, on July 21, Senator Cornyn lifted his hold, when Secretary Clinton promised that the Administration would submit the report and decide on the F-16C/Ds (not necessarily accept the LOR) no later than October 1, 2011.

Meanwhile, the House Foreign Affairs Committee held a hearing on "Why Taiwan Matters," with a non-governmental panel on June 16, 2011, in the first full committee hearing on policy toward Taiwan since 2004. On July 21, the committee completed mark-up of and approved **H.R. 2583**, the Foreign Relations Authorization Act for FY2012, that included an amendment offered by Representatives Connolly, Burton, and Berman to express the sense of Congress that the President should sell and upgrade F-16 fighters as well as sell submarines. On August 1, 181 Members of the House (led by the four co-chairs of the Taiwan Caucus, Representatives Shelley Berkley, Phil Gingrey, Gerald Connolly, and Mario Diaz-Balart) sent a letter to President Obama to urge him to sell all the F-16C/D fighters that Taiwan requires. They requested that the Administration notify Congress of a sale as soon as possible.

On August 15, Representative Ros-Lehtinen, chair of the Foreign Affairs Committee, wrote a letter to Vice President Joe Biden just before his visit to the PRC with arrival in Beijing on August 17, 2011, the 29th anniversary of the August 17, 1982, U.S.-PRC Joint Communique. She warned against discussions with the PRC that would violate the TRA and Six Assurances and urged the Administration to consult with Congress on arms sales to Taiwan. On August 18, Senators Menendez and Inhofe issued a statement to say that it would be unacceptable for President Obama upgrade Taiwan's F-16A/B fighters but not sell new F-16C/D fighters.

In September 2011, the Administration took several long-awaited steps, including responding to Senator Lugar, consulting with Congress, notifying three arms sales programs (including upgrades of existing F-16A/B fighters), and submitting a report on Taiwan's air power. Senator Cornyn introduced **S. 1539**, the Taiwan Airpower Modernization Act of 2011, on September 12, to stipulate that "the President shall carry out the sale of no fewer than 66 F-16C/D multirole fighters to Taiwan." On September 14, Chairwoman Ros-Lehtinen introduced **H.R. 2918**, the Taiwan Policy Act of 2011, which included authorization of a number of possible arms sales, a statement of policy to accept Taiwan's formal letter of request to buy F-16C/D fighters, a requirement for briefings from the Secretary of State in consultation with the Secretary of Defense on potential arms sales, a requirement for an annual report from the President on decision-making on Taiwan's requests, and a requirement for a Presidential report on implementation of security policy under the TRA (including operational planning against a use of force or coercion and the military balance in the Taiwan Strait). Representative Kay Granger introduced **H.R. 2992** on September 21 as the House's version of S. 1539.

On September 20, Senator Cornyn introduced as an amendment to H.R. 2832 his bill to compel a sale of F-16C/Ds. On September 22, the Senate rejected the amendment to the trade bill by a vote of 48-48 with 4 not voting. In a rare floor debate, Senator Cornyn cited the TRA and a memo issued by President Reagan in 1982 which directed that, in quantitative and qualitative terms, Taiwan's defense capability relative to that of the PRC will be maintained, arguing that allowing the cross-strait military disparity is destabilizing to the region, unsettling to allies, and encouraging PRC intimidation. Senators Inhofe and Hutchison expressed support. Senator Max Baucus objected that the amendment would jeopardize the trade bill and free trade agreements with South Korea, Colombia, and Panama. Senator John Kerry expressed opposition, including from the Administration, to the amendment that would risk the free trade agreements and that would compel the President to sell a specific weapon to Taiwan. Senators Feinstein and Boxer also expressed opposition to the amendment, partly for its process to compel a sale of F-16C/Ds. The vote on the amendment did not determine the Senate's intent on a sale of fighters to Taiwan.

While the Administration failed to fulfill part of Secretary Clinton's promise to Senator Cornyn (provide an answer on the F-16C/D fighters), the Administration finally submitted the study on Taiwan's air power by October 1, 2011. Still, only after President Obama already decided to upgrade Taiwan's existing F-16A/B fighters but not give an answer to Congress or Taiwan on new F-16C/D fighters and formally notified Congress on September 21, the Administration submitted on September 22 the Defense Department's comprehensive, classified report on Taiwan's air power. Congress waited about one year for this study that responded to the directive in 2009 (concerning the NDAA for FY2010). The Departments of Defense and State briefed the study to committees in the Senate on September 28 and in the House on October 5.

After President Ma expressed appreciation for the U.S. announcement on September 21, 2011, on the F-16A/B upgrades despite the lack of an answer on F-16C/Ds, Senator Cornyn wrote on September 28 to ask Ma to clarify whether Taiwan still requires 66 new F-16C/D fighters. President Ma did not respond directly but had his Secretary-General reply on October 14 that both F-16A/B upgrades and new F-16C/Ds are needed in qualitative and quantitative terms.

The House Foreign Affairs Committee rescheduled to October 4, 2011, the second part of the hearing on "Why Taiwan Matters" with an official panel. Assistant Secretary of State Kurt Campbell reaffirmed the Six Assurances, stressing the one of no prior consultation with the PRC on arms sales to Taiwan. Acting Assistant Secretary of Defense Peter Lavoy welcomed the initiatives by President Ma Ying-jeou since 2008 to engage closer with the PRC. He testified that the U.S. military relationship with Taiwan has strengthened and enabled the cross-strait warming trend. However, the PLA has not reduced the military threat to Taiwan. He expressed the U.S. concern that a Taiwan that is vulnerable, isolated, and under threat would not be in a position to discuss its future with the mainland and might invite the very aggression we would seek to deter. He warned that if the PLA were to attack, it would be able to rapidly degrade Taiwan's ability to resist. He testified that the Defense Department's report to Congress on Taiwan's air power concluded that Taiwan's defense cannot match the PLA one-for-one. He reiterated the Pentagon's view that Taiwan needs new non-traditional innovative and asymmetric approaches. He warned that Taiwan's lasting security cannot be achieved simply by buying limited numbers of advanced weapons systems. But Lavoy then repeated the Administration's assertion that its decision not to give an answer on new F-16C/Ds and to upgrade Taiwan's existing F-16A/Bs (a traditional, older platform) was a "significant contribution to Taiwan's airpower." In response to Representative Gerry Connolly, Campbell claimed to value consultations between the Executive and Legislative Branches under the TRA and to decide on arms sales without the factor of PRC objections, but did not say why the Administration had no answer on new F-16C/Ds.

On the issue of whether Washington consulted with Beijing, Defense Secretary Leon Panetta said on October 23, 2011, that U.S. officials gave PRC officials a "heads up" about the arms sales. The Administration argued that it did not consult on decisions, but it informed Taiwan's and the PRC's officials after notifying Congress and before announcing the sales to the American people on September 21. On November 7, the four Co-Chairs of the Taiwan Caucus (Representatives Berkley, Gingrey, Connolly, and Diaz-Balart) wrote to Panetta, noting that notification does not explicitly violate the Six Assurances but expecting that notification has not and will not lead to any consultations with the PRC prior to decisions on arms sales to Taiwan.

On November 18, 2011, Senator Cornyn proposed his legislation (to stipulate that the President sell 66 F-16C/D fighters) as S.Amdt. 1200 to S. 1867 (a bill for the NDAA for FY2012). On December 1, Senators McCain and Sessions also voiced support on the floor. The Chairman of the Senate Armed Services Committee ruled that the amendment was non-germane. Although the U.S.-Taiwan Business Council criticized Senator Levin for "blocking" the sale, the actions on Senator Cornyn's amendment did not affect the merits of a sale of F-16C/Ds to Taiwan.

Also on November 18, Senator Cornyn wrote to President Obama, noting his "clear failure" to comply with the TRA, the lack of assistance on the quantitative problem in Taiwan's air force, and the Senator's support for the nominee to be the Assistant Secretary of Defense for Asian and Pacific Security Affairs as linked to a course of action to address Taiwan's fighter shortfall. The President did not respond directly. Acting Under Secretary of Defense for Policy James Miller finally replied on February 15, 2012, noting that the report to Congress on Taiwan's air power concluded that Taiwan's military cannot match the PLA one-for-one. He wrote that the report stressed that Taiwan should plan and procure based on innovative, asymmetric approaches. He contended that the F-16A/B upgrade effectively meets Taiwan's "current needs." Still, he noted the report's acknowledgment that a capable air force is critical and provides deterrence in peacetime. Senator Cornyn then placed a hold on Mark Lippert as President Obama's nominee. Later, in answer to Senator Cornyn's questions at a hearing of the Senate Armed Services Committee on February 28, the PACOM Commander, Admiral Robert Willard, acknowledged that Taiwan's air force still has unmet needs in the long term. Then on April 27, to get Lippert's confirmation, the White House sent a letter to Senator Cornyn, promising to provide "serious consideration" to his proposal on a sale of F-16C/Ds and a "near-term" course of action to address Taiwan's fighter gap, including the sale of an undetermined number of new U.S.-made fighters. On May 17, the House voted (by voice vote) to approve an amendment (as one of amendments en bloc) offered by Representative Granger to **H.R. 4310**, the NDAA for FY2013, to stipulate that the President shall sell at least 66 F-16C/D fighters to Taiwan. The House passed H.R. 4310 on May 18.

# Major U.S. Arms Sales as Notified to Congress

The following table provides information on U.S. sales (not deliveries) of major defense articles and services to Taiwan, as approved by the President and formally notified to Congress since 1990. Based on unclassified notices and news reports, this list includes the date of notification, major item or service proposed for sale, and estimated value of the arms sales program. The list was compiled based on unclassified notifications to Congress or announcements by the Administration as well as press reports. These were primarily government-to-government Foreign Military Sales (FMS) programs. Before the Defense Department may issue Letters of Offer and Acceptance, the President must notify major FMS to Congress as required by Section 36(b) of the Arms Export Control Act (AECA), P.L. 90-629.[250] If 30 calendar days pass after the formal notification and Congress does not pass a joint resolution of disapproval, the Executive Branch is allowed to proceed with the proposed arms sales to Taiwan. Not all of these approved sales were necessarily purchased by Taiwan. There have been other transfers of U.S. defense articles and services not included in this list (that amounted to billions of dollars), including sales and technical assistance with smaller individual values not required to be notified to Congress, those with classified notifications, and Direct Commercial Sales (DCS) licensed for export by the State Department and notified to Congress under Section 36(c) of the AECA (subject to the commercial confidentiality requirements of Section 38(e)). There have been leases of naval vessels and other equipment. Moreover, each year, hundreds of Taiwan's military personnel at different levels receive training and education at U.S. military colleges, academies, and other institutions or units.

### Table 2. Major U.S. Arms Sales as Notified to Congress

| Date of notification | Major item or service as proposed (usually part of a program with related support) | Value of program ($ million) |
|---|---|---|
| **1990** | | |
| 07/26 | Cooperative Logistics Supply Support | $108 |
| 09/06 | (1) C-130H transport aircraft | $45 |
| **1991** | | |
| 01/07 | (100) MK-46 torpedoes | $28 |
| 07/24 | (97) SM-1 Standard air defense missiles | $55 |
| 09/13 | (110) M60A3 tanks | $119 |
| 11/18 | Phase III PIP Mod Kits for HAWK air defense systems | $170 |
| **1992** | | |
| 05/27 | Weapons, ammunition, support for 3 leased ships | $212 |
| 05/27 | Supply support arrangement | $107 |
| 08/04 | (207) SM-1 Standard air defense missiles | $126 |
| 09/14 | (150) F-16A/B fighters | $5,800 |
| 09/14 | (3) Patriot-derived Modified Air Defense System (MADS) fire units[251] | $1,300 |
| 09/18 | (12) SH-2F LAMPS anti-submarine helicopters | $161 |
| **1993** | | |
| 06/17 | (12) C-130H transport aircraft | $620 |

---

[250] As with all U.S. arms sales, months or years *after* the President's decisions on Taiwan's requests and Taiwan's decisions on which sales to pursue, the role of Congress includes informal and formal review of major proposed FMS notified to Congress (during which Congress may enact a joint resolution of disapproval) as stipulated under Section 36(b) of the AECA. See CRS Report RL31675, *Arms Sales: Congressional Review Process*, by Richard F. Grimmett.

[251] Commercial sale. Opall Barbara and David Silverberg, "Taiwanese May Soon Coproduce Patriot," *Defense News*, February 22-28, 1993; *Military Balance 1999-2000.*

| Date of notification | Major item or service as proposed (usually part of a program with related support) | Value of program ($ million) |
|---|---|---|
| 06/25 | Supply support arrangement | $156 |
| 07/29 | (38) Harpoon anti-ship missiles | $68 |
| 07/30 | Logistics support services for 40 leased T-38 trainers | $70 |
| 08/ | (4) E-2T Hawkeye airborne early warning aircraft[252] | $700 |
| 09/08 | Logistics support services for MADS | $175 |
| 11/04 | (150) MK-46 Mod 5 torpedoes | $54 |
| 11/09 | Weapons, ammunition, and support for 3 leased frigates | $238 |
| 11/23 | MK-41 Mod Vertical Launch Systems for ship-based air defense missiles | $103 |
| **1994** | | |
| 08/01 | (80) AN/ALQ-184 electronic counter measure (ECM) pods | $150 |
| 09/12 | MK-45 Mod 2 gun system | $21 |
| **1995** | | |
| 03/24 | (6) MK-75 shipboard gun systems, (6) Phalanx Close-In Weapon Systems | $75 |
| 06/07 | Supply support arrangement | $192 |
| **1996** | | |
| 05/10 | Improved Mobile Subscriber Equipment communications system | $188 |
| 05/10 | (30) TH-67 training helicopters, (30) sets of AN/AVS-6 night vision goggles | $53 |
| 05/23 | (465) Stinger missiles, (55) dual-mounted Stinger launcher systems | $84 |
| 06/24 | (300) M60A3TTS tanks | $223 |
| 08/23 | (1,299) Stinger surface-to-air missiles, (74) Avenger vehicle mounted guided missile launchers, (96) HMMWVs (high-mobility multi-purpose wheeled vehicle) | $420 |
| 09/05 | (110) MK-46 MOD 5 anti-submarine torpedoes | $66 |
| **1997** | | |
| 02/14 | (54) Harpoon anti-ship missiles | $95 |
| 05/23 | (1,786) TOW 2A anti-armor guided missiles, (114) TOW launchers, (100) HMMWVs | $81 |
| 07/24 | (21) AH-1W Super Cobra helicopters[253] | $479 |
| 09/03 | (13) OH-58D Kiowa Warrior Armed Scout helicopters | $172 |
| 11/09 | Pilot training and logistics support for F-16 fighters | $280 |
| 11/09 | Spare parts for various aircraft | $140 |
| **1998** | | |
| 01/28 | (3) Knox-class frigates,[254] (1) MK 15 Phalanx Close-In Weapons System | $300 |

[252] *Flight International*, September 1-7, 1993.

[253] Taiwan reportedly ordered 63 AH-1W helicopters, 42 of which were delivered by early 2000, and Taiwan may order an additional 24 helicopters (*Defense News*, March 6, 2000).

[254] In 1992, the Bush Administration submitted legislation that Congress passed to lease three Knox-class frigates to (continued...)

| Date of notification | Major item or service as proposed (usually part of a program with related support) | Value of program ($ million) |
|---|---|---|
| 06/01 | (28) Pathfinder/Sharpshooter navigation and targeting pods for F-16 fighters[255] | $160 |
| 08/27 | (58) Harpoon anti-ship missiles | $101 |
| 08/27 | (61) Dual-mount Stinger surface-to-air missiles | $180 |
| 08/27 | (131) MK 46 Mod 5(A)S anti-submarine torpedoes | $69 |
| 10/09 | (9) CH-47SD Chinook helicopters | $486 |
| **1999** | | |
| 05/26 | (240) AGM-114KS Hellfire II air-to-surface missiles | $23 |
| 05/26 | (5) AN/VRC-92E SINCGARS radio systems, (5) Intelligence Electronic Warfare systems, (5) HMMWVs | $64 |
| 07/30 | Spare parts for F-5E/F, C-130H, F-16A/B, and IDF aircraft | $150 |
| 07/30 | (2) E-2T Hawkeye 2000E airborne early warning aircraft | $400 |
| **2000** | | |
| 03/02 | Modernization of the TPS-43F air defense radar to TPS-75V configuration | $96 |
| 03/02 | (162) HAWK Intercept guided air defense missiles | $106 |
| 06/07 | (39) Pathfinder/Sharpshooter navigation and targeting pods for F-16 fighters | $234 |
| 06/07 | (48) AN/ALQ-184 ECM pods for F-16s | $122 |
| 09/28 | (146) M109A5 howitzers, 152 SINCGARS radio systems | $405 |
| 09/28 | (200) AIM-120C AMRAAMs for F-16 fighters | $150 |
| 09/28 | (71) RGM-84L Harpoon anti-ship missiles | $240 |
| 09/28 | Improved Mobile Subscriber Equipment (IMSE) communication system | $513 |
| **2001** | | |
| 07/18 | (50) Joint Tactical Information Distribution Systems (JTIDS) terminals (a version of Link 16) for data links between aircraft, ships, and ground stations | $725 |
| 09/05 | (40) AGM-65G Maverick air-to-ground missiles for F-16s | $18 |
| 10/26 | (40) Javelin anti-tank missile systems and (360) Javelin missiles | $51 |
| 10/30 | Logistical support/spare parts for F-5E/F, C-130H, F-16A/B, and IDF aircraft | $288 |
| **2002** | | |
| 06/04 | (3) AN/MPN-14 air traffic control radars | $108 |
| 09/04 | (54) AAV7A1 amphibious assault vehicles | $250 |
| 09/04 | Maintenance and spare parts for aircraft, radars, AMRAAMS, other systems | $174 |
| 09/04 | (182) AIM-9M-1/2 Sidewinder air-to-air missiles | $36 |
| 09/04 | (449) AGM-114M3 Hellfire II anti-armor missiles to equip AH-1W and OH-58D helicopters | $60 |

---

(...continued)

Taiwan. Taiwan leased a total of six (and bought them in 1999) and purchased two in 1998 (plus one for spares).

[255] The sale of the navigation/targeting pods excluded the laser designator feature, but the Pentagon notified Congress on May 16, 2000, that 20 sets would be upgraded to include the feature.

| Date of notification | Major item or service as proposed (usually part of a program with related support) | Value of program ($ million) |
|---|---|---|
| 10/11 | (290) TOW-2B anti-tank missiles | $18 |
| 11/21 | (4) Kidd-class destroyers | $875 |
| **2003** | | |
| 09/24 | Multi-functional Information Distribution Systems (MIDS) (for Po Sheng) | $775 |
| **2004** | | |
| 03/30 | (2) Ultra High Frequency Long Range Early Warning Radars | $1,776 |
| **2005** | | |
| 10/25 | (10) AIM-9M Sidewinder and (5) AIM-7M Sparrow air-to-air missiles; continued pilot training and logistical support for F-16 fighters at Luke AFB | $280 |
| **2007** | | |
| 02/28 | (218) AMRAAMs and (235) Maverick air-to-ground missiles for F-16 fighters | $421 |
| 08/08 | (60) AGM-84L Harpoon Block II anti-ship missiles | $125 |
| 09/12 | (144) SM-2 Block IIIA Standard air-defense missiles for Kidd-class destroyers | $272 |
| 09/12 | (12) P-3C maritime patrol/ASW aircraft | $1,960 |
| 11/09 | Patriot configuration 2 ground systems upgrade | $939 |
| **2008** | | |
| 10/3 | (330) Patriot Advanced Capability (PAC)-3 missile defense missiles | $3,100 |
| 10/3 | (32) UGM-84L sub-launched Harpoon anti-ship missiles | $200 |
| 10/3 | spare parts for F-5E/F, C-130H, F-16A/B, IDF aircraft | $334 |
| 10/3 | (182) Javelin anti-armor missiles | $47 |
| 10/3 | upgrade of (4) E-2T aircraft (Hawkeye 2000 configuration) | $250 |
| 10/3 | (30) AH-64D Apache Longbow attack helicopters | $2,532 |
| **2010** | | |
| 01/29 | (114) PAC-3 missile defense missiles | $2,810 |
| 01/29 | (60) UH-60M Black Hawk utility helicopters | $3,100 |
| 01/29 | (12) Harpoon Block II anti-ship telemetry (training) missiles | $37 |
| 01/29 | (60) MIDS (follow-on technical support for Po Sheng C4 systems) | $340 |
| 01/29 | (2) Osprey-class mine hunting ships (refurbished and upgraded) | $105 |
| **2011** | | |
| 09/21 | Retrofit of 145 F-16A/B fighters, with 176 AESA radars, JDAMs, etc. | $5,300 |
| 09/21 | Continuation of training of F-16 pilots at Luke Air Force Base | $500 |
| 09/21 | Spare parts for F-16A/B, F-5E/F, C-130H, and IDF aircraft | $52 |

# Author Contact Information

Shirley A. Kan
Specialist in Asian Security Affairs
skan@crs.loc.gov, 7-7606

www.ingramcontent.com/pod-product-compliance
Lightning Source LLC
Chambersburg PA
CBHW081606170526
45166CB00009B/2848